NEW

CUTTING
EDGE

PRE-INTERMEDIATE

WORKBOOK

T0385899

jane comyns carr   sarah cunningham

peter moor

PEARSON

Longman

CONTENTS

Introduction

	PAGE
Grammar terms	4

Module 1

Question forms: Word order	5
Question words	6
Subject and object questions	6
Present simple	7
Short answers	8
Frequency: Adverbs	8
Frequency: Phrases	8
Vocabulary booster: Sports	9
Vocabulary: Leisure activities	10
Phrases with *go and play*	10
Real life: Questions you can't live without	10
Pronunciation: The /ə/ sound	11
Improve your writing: Punctuation	11

Module 2

Past simple: Regular and irregular verbs	12
Negatives and affirmatives	13
did, was or *were* in questions and answers	13
Time phrases often used in the past: *ago*	14
in, at, on	14
Vocabulary: Words to describe feelings	14
Vocabulary booster: TV programmes	15
Listen and read: TV classics	16
Wordspot: *feel*	17
Spelling: *-ed* endings	17
Pronunciation: Irregular verbs	17
Improve your writing: Linkers: *but, so, because, then*	17

Module 3

should/shouldn't	18
can/can't	18
have to / don't have to	18
can/can't, have to / don't have to	19
Short answers with modal verbs: *should, can, have to*	19
Vocabulary: Daily routine	20
Vocabulary: Jobs	20
Listen and read: The secrets of sleep	21
Real life: Making requests and asking for permission	21
Vocabulary booster: Studying	22
Pronunciation: The letter 'a'	23
Improve your writing: Writing a paragraph	23
Spelling: Finding mistakes	23

Module 4

	PAGE
Present continuous	24
State and action verbs	24
Present simple or Present continuous?	24
Present continuous for future arrangements	25
Vocabulary: Special occasions	26
Real life: Phrases for special occasions	26
Wordspot: *day*	26
Vocabulary booster: Special occasions	27
Listen and read: Religious festivals around the world	28
Improve your writing: A letter of invitation	29
Spelling: *-ing* forms	29
Pronunciation: /ð/ and /θ/	29

Module 5

Comparative and superlative adjectives:	
Comparative forms	30
Superlative forms	30
Prepositions in comparative phrases: *as, than, from, like, in, to*	31
Making comparisons with nouns	31
Describing people: Questions about appearance	31
is or has got?	32
That's him!	32
Order of adjectives	33
Vocabulary: Adjectives to describe appearance	33
Vocabulary: Physical appearance	33
Vocabulary booster: Parts of the face and body	34
Wordspot: *look*	35
Pronunciation: The letter 'o'	35
Improve your writing: Writing a description	35

Module 6

Intentions and wishes: *going to, planning to, would like to, would rather:* Positive and negative forms	36
Question forms	36
Predictions: *will* and *won't*	37
Short answers with *will, won't* and *going to*	38
Pronunciation: *'ll, will* and *won't*	38
Real life: Social chit-chat	38
Vocabulary: Holidays	39
Vocabulary booster: Things you take on holiday	39
Listen and read: Holiday offers	40
Improve your writing: More postcards	41
Spelling: Words ending with *-ed* and *-ing*	41

Module 7

Present perfect: Positive, negative and question forms	42
Present perfect and Past simple with *for*	42
Present perfect: Short answers	42
Present perfect with *just, yet, already,* and *never*	43
Present perfect and Past simple with time phrases	43
been or *gone*	43
Present perfect and Past simple	44
Past participles wordsearch	44
Vocabulary: ambitions and dreams	45
Pronunciation: The sounds /æ/ and /ʌ/	45
Vocabulary booster: Celebrity jobs	46
Wordspot: *for*	46
Improve your writing: A mini-biography	47

Module 8

	PAGE
Using articles: *a* or *the*	48
Zero for general statements	48
For general and specific statements	48
With geographical features	49
Phrases without *the*	49
Quantifiers with countable and uncountable nouns:	
some, any and *no*	50
much, many, a lot, a few, no	50
much, many, too much, too many and *not enough*	51
Vocabulary: Geographical features	51
Vocabulary booster: Things you find in cities	51
Listen and read: Volcanoes	52
Pronunciation: Compounds with two nouns	53
Real life: Asking for and giving directions	53
Improve your writing: Notes giving directions	53
Spelling: Same pronunciation, different spelling	
(homophones)	53

Module 9

may, might, will, definitely, **etc.:** *will/won't*	54
will probably / probably won't	54
may/might	55
will/won't/may/might	55
Present tense after *if, when, before* **and other time**	
words: Present tense after *if*	56
Time clauses: *if, when, before, as soon as*	56
Word order	57
Vocabulary: Modern and traditional	57
Pronunciation: The letter 'i'	57
Vocabulary booster: Technology	58
Wordspot: *if*	59
Improve your writing: Saying thank you	59

Module 10

used to: *used to / didn't use to*	60
Past continuous: Important moments in history	60
Past continuous and Past simple	61
Questions and short answers	62
Vocabulary: Health and accidents	62
Vocabulary: Verb + noun/adjective combinations	62
Vocabulary booster: At the doctor's	63
Listen and read: Flying doctors	64
Pronunciation: The letter 'c'	65
Improve your writing: Time phrases	65

Module 11

Gerunds (*-ing* forms) after verbs of liking and	
disliking	66
Gerunds after prepositions	66
Verbs of liking and disliking	67
like doing and *would like to do*	67
Would you like ...? and *Do you like ...?*: short answers	68
Vocabulary: Hobbies and interests	68
Vocabulary booster: *-ed* and *-ing* adjectives	69
Wordspot: *like*	70
Spelling: Words ending with *-ion*	70
Pronunciation: Words ending with *-ion*	70
Improve your writing: Replying to invitations	71

Module 12

	PAGE
Passive forms: Identifying passive forms	72
Present simple passive	72
Questions	73
Active or passive?	73
Past simple passive	74
Questions	74
Listen and read: Diamonds are forever	75
Vocabulary: Everyday objects	76
Spelling / Pronunciation: Silent 'g' and 'gh'	76
Real life: Making suggestions	76
Vocabulary booster: Outdoor equipment	77

Module 13

Present perfect continuous	78
Time phrases with *for* and *since*	78
Present perfect with *for* and *since*	78
Present perfect continuous and Present perfect	
simple: Stative verbs	79
Reading: Jobsearch.com	80
Vocabulary: Personal characteristics	82
Wordspot: *how*	82
Pronunciation: Some 'hard to pronounce' words	83
Improve your writing: Error correction (1)	83

Module 14

Past perfect	84
Past perfect and Past simple	84
Irregular past forms	84
Past time words: *already, just, never ... before*	85
Past time words: Past perfect or Present perfect?	85
Vocabulary: Money	86
Vocabulary: Prepositions	86
Vocabulary booster: Shopping	87
Wordspot: *make*	87
Pronunciation: The sounds /eɪ/ and /e/	87
Listen and read: Money	88
Real life: Dealing with money	89
Improve your writing: Paying online	89

Module 15

Conditional sentences with would: *would* and	
wouldn't	90
might or *would*	90
will and *would*	91
Short answers with *will* and *would*	91
Vocabulary booster: People in politics, religion and	
public life	92
Listen and read: The planets	93
Spelling: Silent 'w'	94
Pronunciation: The sound /w/	94
Improve your writing: Error correction (2)	94
Pronunciation table	95

Grammar terms

1 Use the words in the box to describe the words in bold below.

adjective   article (indefinite)   noun (countable)
pronoun   adverb   auxiliary verb
noun (uncountable)   main verb   article (definite)
possessive adjective   modal verb   preposition

a   an **old** woman
    a **good** film
    a **small** country   _adjective_

b   **my** family
    your name
    his friends   _____

c   **I** like coffee.
    Where are **you** from?
    Do **you** know **her**?   _____

d   **Can** you swim?
    It **might** rain tonight.
    Could you open the door?   _____

e   Speak **slowly**.
    Come back **tomorrow**.
    He's **always** late.   _____

f   **Have** you finished?
    What time **does** she arrive?
    It **will** be cold tomorrow.   _____

g   The film **starts** at ten.
    Do you **speak** English?
    How do you **spell** it?   _____

h   a **cat**
    an **elephant**
    eggs   _____

i   **the** Internet
    the time
    the President   _____

j   **money**
    weather
    homework   _____

k   They're **from** Brazil
    at eight o'clock
    in the kitchen   _____

l   **a** house
    an orange
    a book   _____

2 Look at the song titles below. Find an example of:

a   an auxiliary verb   _do_
b   an adjective   _____
c   an indefinite article   _____
d   a countable noun   _____
e   a pronoun   _____
f   an adverb   _____
g   an uncountable noun   _____
h   a main verb   _____
i   a modal verb   _____
j   a possessive adjective   _____

Do you Want to Know a Secret?

Your Kiss Is Sweet

You Can Never Stop My Love

You Might See Me Cry

BOYS WANT TO HAVE FUN

I Will Always Love You

Question forms
Word order

1 a Michael Aarons, World 100 metres Champion, is in Rome for an important athletics meeting. Write the journalists' questions by putting the words in the correct order.

1 first time / this / Is / here in Rome / your ?
   Is this your first time here in Rome?

   No. I first came here about eight years ago.

2 your family / with / here / Is / you ?
   _____?

   My wife is here; my children are with their grandparents in the United States.

3 enjoy / wife / Does / athletics / your ?
   _____?

   She says so, but I think she's really here because she likes shopping!

4 life / you / here in Italy / like / Do ?
   _____?

   Of course, especially the food and the sunshine!

5 you / about / the Italian champion, Giacomo Zanetti / Are / worried ?
   _____?

   Giacomo is a great athlete and a good friend ... but I think I can win!

6 you / Do / have / for young athletes / any advice ?
   _____?

   Sure – train hard, live a healthy life, and you can be a champion too!

b **T1.1** Listen and check.

Question words

2 Use each question word **once** to complete the questions about Parcheesi – the national game of India.

Parcheesi! The national game of India

| how | how long | where | which | who | why |
| how many | what | ~~what kind~~ | when | | |

a   _What kind_ of game is Parcheesi?

It's a board game – like chess or backgammon.

b   _____ country does it come from originally?

India.

c   _____ do people play it now?

All over the world – it's very popular in the USA.

d   _____ does 'Parcheesi' mean?

It comes from 'pacis', which means twenty-five.

e   _____ did people start playing it?

Hundreds of years ago: but it only came to Europe in the nineteenth century.

f   _____ invented it?

Nobody knows!

g   _____ people can play?

Four.

h   _____ do you play?

By moving all your pieces to the centre of the board.

i   _____ does a game last?

Usually about half an hour.

j   _____ is it so popular?

Because it's easy to learn ... but difficult to play well!

Subject and object questions

There are two different types of question with *who* (and *what*).

a *Who* is the subject of the sentence:

subject

Who *is* speaking?   **no** inversion of subject and verb

b *Who* is the object of the sentence:

object	subject

Who *are you* *speaking to?*   inversion of subject and verb

In the Present (and Past) simple we do **not** use *do/did* in subject questions:

Who **knows** the answer?
~~Who does know the answer?~~

What **happened**?
~~What did happen?~~

3 Decide if *who* is the subject or object of the questions below. Circle the correct form.

a   Who (wants) / *does want* a cup of coffee?

b   Who *won / did win* the football match last night?

c   Who *want / do you want* to go with?

d   Who *knows / does know* the right answer?

e   Who *already know / do you already know* in this class?

f   Who *told / did tell* you the news?

g   Who *live / do you live* with?

h   Who *lives / does live* in the flat next door?

i   Who *smokes / does smoke*?

j   Who *broke / did break* my pen?

k   Who *did phone / did you phone* just now?

l   Who *went / did you go* out with last night?

m   Who *gave you / did you give* those chocolates?

n   What *happens / does happen* at the end of the film?

Present simple

4 **a** Read the text about the Wilson sisters.

Jennifer and Rosemary Wilson are twin sisters, and they're both famous ... but they have very different lives!

Jennifer lives in London: she's a well-known TV presenter, and she gets up at 3 a.m. every day to introduce the popular breakfast TV show *Good Morning UK!* She finishes work at about 10.30 a.m.

Rosemary is a professional tennis player: she now lives in Beverley Hills, USA with her American husband, Ron. Rosemary comes to England two or three times a year to play: she always stays with her sister.

b Correct the information in the sentences below. Use the information in the text.

1 Jennifer and Rosemary have very similar lives.
   They don't have very similar lives, they have very different lives.

2 Jennifer and Rosemary live in the same country.
   _____
   _____

3 Jennifer lives in the United States.
   _____
   _____

4 She works in the evening.
   _____
   _____

5 Rosemary plays golf.
   _____
   _____

6 She stays in a hotel when she comes to Britain.
   _____
   _____
   _____
   _____

7 They see each other every weekend.
   _____
   _____
   _____
   _____
   _____

c Write questions.

1 *Where does Jennifer Wilson live?*
   She lives in London.

2 _____ ?
   At 3 a.m.

3 _____ ?
   At about 10.30 a.m.

4 _____ ?
   In Beverley Hills.

5 _____ ?
   Two or three times a year.

6 _____ ?
   To play tennis.

7 _____ ?
   With her sister.

d **T1.2** Listen and check. Practise the pronunciation of the questions.

Short answers

> **LOOK!**
>
> When we answer questions, we often use short answers, like this:
>
> | Question | Short answer | | |
> |---|---|---|---|
> | **Do you** / **they** play tennis? | Yes, **I** / **they do**. | or | No, **I** / **they don't**. |
> | **Does (s)he** like ice cream? | Yes **(s)he does**. | or | No, **(s)he doesn't**. |

5 a Answer these questions about yourself. Use short answers.

1 Do you like pasta?   *Yes, I do.*

2 Do you live near the sea?   _____

3 Do you smoke?   _____

b Answer these questions about someone you know well (for example, your mother or your best friend). Use short answers.

1 Does he/she wear glasses?   _____

2 Does he/she live near you?   _____

3 Does he/she drive a car?   _____

c Answer these questions about Jennifer and Rosemary Wilson. Read the text again if necessary. Use short answers.

1 Do they live in the same city?   _____

2 Do they have the same job?   _____

3 Do they often visit each other?   _____

4 Do they look similar?   _____

Frequency Adverbs

6 Complete each sentence with a frequency adverb so it is true for you. Be careful to put the adverb in the correct position in the sentence.

always	often	sometimes	occasionally	never

sometimes
a I /\ watch TV in bed.

b I am late for work/school.

c I play computer games.

d I go to the opera.

e I cook a meal for my friends.

f I eat chocolate.

Phrases

> **LOOK!**
>
> | once twice three times four times, etc. | a | day week month year |
> |---|---|---|

7 Replace the phrase in bold with a frequency phrase. Use the word in brackets to help you.

a I go to English lessons **on Tuesdays and Thursdays.**
I go to English lessons
twice a week . (week)

b We usually go on holiday **in April, in July and in December.**
We usually go on holiday
_____ . (year)

c We go swimming **every Sunday.**
We go swimming
_____ . (week)

d It's important to visit the dentist **every six months.**
It's important to visit the dentist
_____ . (year)

e My friend goes running **on Mondays, Wednesdays, Fridays and Sundays.**
My friend goes running
_____ . (week)

f I check my e-mail **in the morning and in the evening.**
I check my e-mail
_____ . (day)

g I go to visit my cousin in Bristol **about every four weeks.**
I go to visit my cousin in Bristol
_____ . (month)

Vocabulary booster: sports

8 **a** What are the sports and activities below? Use the pictures to help you.

1	s e l l a b b a	b a s e b a l l
2	y c c i l g n	_ _ _ _ _ _ _
3	i n k s i g	_ _ _ _ _ _
4	g w i m s m i n	_ _ _ _ _ _ _ _
5	c i e - i t a n k s g	_ _ _ - _ _ _ _ _ _
6	e s h o r - i d n g i r	_ _ _ _ - _ _ _ _ _
7	b l e a t n i n s e t	_ _ _ _ _ _ _ _ _ _
8	l e b l a k t a b s	_ _ _ _ _ _ _ _ _
9	g o b n i x	_ _ _ _ _ _
10	m i s t c a n g y s	_ _ _ _ _ _ _ _ _
11	l o b v a l e l y l	_ _ _ _ _ _ _ _ _
12	u j o d	_ _ _ _
13	d o s n i b r g w o a n	_ _ _ _ _ _ _ _ _ _ _
14	g u r y b	_ _ _ _ _
15	b r a k t s e o g d n i a	_ _ _ _ _ _ _ _ _ _ _ _

b **T1.3** Listen to the spelling and pronunciation of the words. Practise the pronunciation.

c Write the names of:

1 **one** sport which needs gloves. __boxing__

2 **five** sports which use a ball. _____
_____ _____ _____ _____

3 **four** sports which need water, ice or snow.
_____ _____ _____ _____

4 **four** sports in which you ride on something.
_____ _____ _____ _____

5 **three** sports you do in a gym. _____
_____ _____

6 **two** sports in which you have one opponent.
_____ _____

7 **four** sports for which you often have a referee.
_____ _____ _____ _____

Vocabulary
Leisure activities

9 **a** Complete the phrases with a verb from the box.

| do | eat | get | go for a | listen to | read | rent |
| watch | | | | | | |

1 _rent_   a DVD
          a video
2 _____   a magazine
          a newspaper
3 _____   in
          out
4 _____   some exercise
          fit
5 _____   music
          the radio
6 _____   walk
          run
7 _____   yoga
          an activity
8 _____   a film
          a match

b Complete the sentences with the correct form of the verbs in part **a**.

1 My boss __reads__ a newspaper every day.
2 My cousin _____ yoga every morning before breakfast.
3 I never _____ DVDs: I prefer to go to the cinema.
4 Do you _____ the radio in the car?
5 What can I do to _____ fit?
6 Do you prefer to _____ a football match live, or on TV?
7 My colleague and I sometimes _____ run after work.
8 We _____ out two or three times a month at our favourite Greek restaurant.

Phrases with *go* and *play*

go	+	activity (= verb + **-ing**)	go skiing
go to the	+	place	go to the gym
play	+	sport/game	play football, play cards
play the	+	musical instrument	play the guitar

LOOK!

10 Put the words in the box in the correct column.

chess	gym	football	guitar	cinema
table tennis	violin	park	computer games	
shopping	beach	skiing	ice-skating	trumpet
piano	dancing			

go	go to the	play	play the
		chess	

Real life
Questions you can't live without

11 Correct the mistakes in the questions.

a I can help you?
   Can I help you?
b How much is this cost?
   _____
c What time is?
   _____
d When's your date of birth?
   _____
e Where do you from?
   _____
f Where is the toilets, please?
   _____
g How do you spelling your name?
   _____
h Sorry, you repeat that, please?
   _____
i Where part of Turkey are you from?
   _____
j Where's nearest post office?
   _____
k How long time are you going to stay?
   _____
l You speak English?
   _____

Pronunciation
The /ə/ sound

The word *teacher* has two syllables:
    teach·er
        /ə/
The **first** syllable is stressed (it is stronger and louder).
The **second** syllable is unstressed. We often pronounce unstressed syllables: /ə/.

The word *Internet* has three syllables:
In·ter·net
    /ə/
The **first** syllable is stressed.
The **second** syllable is pronounced: /ə/

12 **a** **T1.4** Listen to the words below. Notice the stress on each word. Write /ə/ under the syllable or syllables which are pronounced /ə/.

1	nev·er	8	foot·bal·ler
2	am·bi·tion	9	pop·u·lar
3	com·put·er	10	re·fe·ree
4	ex·er·cise	11	exc·e·llent
5	yo·ga	12	o·ppo·nent
6	pro·fes·sion·al	13	oft·en
7	lei·sure	14	te·rri·fic

b Listen again and practise the pronunciation of the words.

Improve your writing
Punctuation

A B C D	capital	We use these for the initial letters of: names of people, towns, countries, languages, and at the beginning of a sentence. *My brother Frank teaches English in Italy.*
.	full stop	We use this at the end of a sentence⊙ *... end of a sentence.*
,	a comma	**a** We use this to separate things in a list: *She likes eating out, films, music and dancing.* (before the last item, we use *and* instead of a comma) **b** We also use a comma to show a short pause: *... in Sydney, the biggest city in Australia, you ...*
'	apostrophe	We use this to show contracted forms, and with possessive s: *I'm twenty-six years old.* *When's she arriving?* *We've got a dog and two cats.* *Zoe's friends are in Barcelona.*

13 In the paragraph below:
a put a full stop, comma or an apostrophe in the spaces marked _.
b change twenty letters into capital letters.

'everybody thinks I_m a typical englishwoman,' actress kate thomson told *Go!* magazine. 'I really don_t know why ...'. when she was eighteen_ kate left england_ she lived first in canada_ then morocco_ where she met french film producer serge roux_ the couple now live in paris with their three children: patrick_ james and lucie_ 'We_re so happy here. It_s nice to have children who can speak both english and french_'

MODULE 2

Past simple
Regular and irregular verbs

1 Complete the past forms of the verbs below. Use the list on page 157 of the Students' Book to find out which verbs are irregular.

appear	appear _e_ _d_
drive	dr _ ve
go	we _ _
make	ma _ _
begin	beg _ n
eat	_ t _
happen	happen _ _
meet	m _ _
buy	bou _ _ t
fall	fe _ _
know	kn _ w
play	play _ _
come	c _ me
feel	fe _ _
live	liv _ _
read	r _ _ d
cost	c _ st
find	f _ _ nd
look	look _ _
take	t _ _ k
die	di _ _
get	g _ t
lose	lo _ _
write	wr _ te
invent	invent _ _
think	tho _ _ _ t
forget	forg _ _
stay	stay _ _
sing	s _ ng

2 Put the verbs in brackets into the Past simple.

The First TV Soap Opera

soap op·e·ra /ˈ. ,.../ *n* [C] a television or radio story about the daily lives of the same group of people, which is broadcast regularly

The first TV soap opera (a) __*appeared*__ (appear) on American television just after the Second World War. Its name (b) _____ (be) *Faraway Hill* and it (c) _____ (begin) on 2nd October 1946. A famous Broadway actress, Flora Campbell, (d) _____ (play) Karen St. John, a rich New York woman who (e) _____ (go) to live with her relatives in the country after her husband (f) _____ (die). She soon (g) _____ (meet) a handsome young farmer, and of course the two immediately (h) _____ (fall) in love. Unfortunately, the farmer (i) _____ (be) already engaged to Karen's cousin, who (j) _____ (know) nothing about the relationship. When she (k) _____ (find) out, things (l) _____ (get) very, very difficult for Karen. The producers of *Faraway Hill* (m) _____ (have) very little money – each programme (n) _____ (cost) only $300 – so they (o) _____ (make) them as quickly as possible. Because there (p) _____ (be) no time for the actors to learn their words each week, assistants (q) _____ (write) them on blackboards. Because of this, they often (r) _____ (look) into the distance with a strange, romantic expression on their faces ... as they (s) _____ (read) their words from the boards on the other side of the studio!

Negatives and affirmatives

3 Correct these sentences about *Faraway Hill*.

a The first TV soap opera appeared before the Second World War.
   It didn't appear before the Second World War, it appeared after the Second World War.

b It began in October 1936.
   _____
   _____
   _____
   _____

c It was about a rich farmer who moved to New York.
   _____
   _____
   _____
   _____

d The woman fell in love with her cousin.
   _____
   _____
   _____
   _____

e Her lover was married to her cousin.
   _____
   _____
   _____
   _____

f The producers of the programme had a lot of money.
   _____
   _____
   _____
   _____

g The assistants wrote the actors' words on pieces of paper.
   _____
   _____
   _____
   _____

did, *was* or *were* in questions and answers

4 Yesterday evening Ruth had her first date with Oliver. Her younger sister, Emma, is asking her about it.

a Complete Ruth and Emma's conversation with *was/wasn't*, *were/weren't* or *did/didn't*.

E: So how (1) ___was___ your evening with Oliver?

R: It (2) _____ good. Yes, very good.

E: Mm ... where (3) _____ you go?

R: To see the new James Bond film.

E: (4) _____ it good?

R: Well, it (5) _____ really the kind of film I like, you know, I'm not a James Bond fan, but it (6) _____ quite funny.

E: And (7) _____ you go anywhere after that?

R: We went to that new bar opposite the cinema – a few of Oliver's friends (8) _____ there.

E: (9) _____ they nice?

R: The boy, James, (10) _____ quite nice, but the two girls (11) _____ very friendly – they (12) _____ talk to me at all, not a word.

E: That (13) _____ very nice! How rude!

R: But, anyway, they (14) _____ stay long – they left after about twenty minutes ... and then we stayed and talked for an hour or two ... he (15) _____ really, really funny!

E: Mm, very nice! (16) _____ he buy you dinner?

R: No ... but he bought me a few drinks ...

E: Mm, and (17) _____ he bring you home in his new sports car?

R: Yes ... why?

E: So, (18) _____ he very romantic?

R: Emma, mind your own business!

E: And (19) _____ he ask to see you again?

R: Yes, he (20) _____ , actually ... now go away!

E: Mm ... very interesting!

b **T2.1** Listen and check.

Time phrases often used in the past

ago

5 Answer at least **six** questions below about yourself. Use *ago* in your answers.

a   When did you first start learning English?

I first started learning English three years ago.

b   When did you first learn to write?

_____

c   When did you first use a computer?

_____

d   When did you first send an e-mail?

_____

e   When did you first go abroad?

_____

f   When did you last watch or listen to the news?

_____

g   When did you last make a phone call?

_____

h   When did you last wash your hands?

_____

i   When did you last watch a film?

_____

j   When did you last write a letter to a friend?

_____

in, at, on

6 Complete the gaps with *in*, *at*, *on* or –.

a   My grandmother was born ____*in*____ 1939.

b   I'll meet you at the cinema _____ 8.30.

c   I met Kerry in the street _____ last week – she looked very well.

d   My mother-in-law usually comes to stay _____ Christmas.

e   I've got a doctor's appointment _____ Friday morning.

f   My cat sleeps on my bed _____ night.

g   Pip often goes abroad _____ the winter.

h   Bob moved to New York _____ the 1970s.

Vocabulary
Words to describe feelings

7 Choose one of the adjectives from the box on page 19 of the Students' Book to complete the sentences below.

a   When Amanda didn't come home from her night out, her parents felt very ___*worried*___ .

b   The night before her birthday, Anna was so _____ she couldn't sleep.

c   After a terrible day at work, I got home, listened to some music and had a bath. Then I felt more _____ .

d   I wanted a new DVD player for my birthday, but all I got was a stupid computer game. I was really _____ .

e   OK, OK, I'm nearly ready to go. Don't be so _____ !

f   It was a beautiful sunny day, and as I walked to work, I was _____ .

g   The film was nearly three hours long. A lot of people got _____ and left before the end.

h   I was _____ to see David in London: I thought he was in Paris!

i   Frank woke up and heard a noise downstairs. He was so _____ he couldn't move.

j   My new hair cut looked horrible: I was too _____ to go out.

k   I'm sorry. I lost the CD you lent me. Please don't be _____ .

l   People often feel a little _____ before an important exam.

Vocabulary booster: TV programmes

8 a Which TV programmes are the sentences below about? Write the number next to the word in the box.

a cartoon _____	a soap opera _____	a comedy _____
a drama _____	a sports programme _____	the news _____
a game show _____	a documentary _____	a talk show _____
a cookery programme _____		

1 You can win a lot of money, but I wouldn't like to do it, I'd be too nervous!
2 It's on about four times a day. I usually watch it at nine or ten o'clock.
3 My favourite is Mickey Mouse, but my brother likes *The Simpsons*.
4 I learnt how to make a delicious fish and rice dish the other day.
5 It was about all the dangerous spiders that live in Australia: very scary!
6 I stayed up late to watch the match, and my team lost!
7 It made me laugh and put me in a really good mood.
8 It has famous people who answer questions and talk about themselves.
9 My sister always watches it when she comes home from school. She wants to be like Kelly, the Randles' teenage daughter.
10 It was an interesting story, and the actors were really good, but I didn't like the sad ending: I cried and cried.

b Answer the questions.

1 Which types of programme can you also see at the cinema?

_____

2 In which types of programme are all the people actors?

_____

3 Which types of programme do you watch regularly?

_____

4 Which types of programme do you never watch?

_____

Listen and read

9 a Read and listen to the text about TV classics.

TV Classics

What are the most popular TV programmes in your country? Here are five classic TV programmes which are famous in many parts of the world.

Baywatch

Internationally, *Baywatch* is the most popular TV show in history. *Baywatch* has appeared in 148 countries in every continent – except Antarctica! – which means that about one half of the world's population has seen it at some time. From its first episode in 1989, this TV drama had everything: beautiful young men and women in swimming costumes, fantastic sunshine and perfect California beaches. And it wasn't just men who liked it. Sixty-five percent of the people watching it were female.

Walking with Dinosaurs

Walking with Dinosaurs first appeared on British television in 1999. Using modern computer technology, it showed dinosaurs walking, eating, sleeping and fighting sixty-five million years before TV! The series cost six million pounds and it took three years to make. Some scientists said that the programme invented facts about how the dinosaurs lived, but that wasn't a problem for the millions of people who watched it. When it appeared on *The Discovery Channel*, it became the most popular documentary programme ever on cable TV. The series has appeared in more than ninety countries.

Pop Idol

In 2001, British music boss Simon Cowell had the idea of a TV 'talent show' for members of the public who wanted to be pop singers. Thousands of singers – good and bad – appeared in front of three judges and TV viewers could vote for the best ten by telephone, text message or over the Internet. The idea was a big success internationally, and the United States soon had its own *American Idol*. Similar shows appeared all over the world, from Russia to the Arab world. Diana Karzon, nineteen, from Jordan won the first *Arab Super Star* in August 2004.

Fawlty Towers

In this classic British comedy of the 1970s, John Cleese plays Basil Fawlty, the owner of a hotel in a small town by the sea. Basil is always angry: angry with his wife, Sybil, angry with the people who work in his hotel (including Manuel, the waiter from Spain) and even angry with the hotel guests. The last episode of *Fawlty Towers* appeared more than thirty years ago, but you can still see this classic British comedy all over the world.

Big Brother

Some people loved it, some people hated it, but one thing is certain: *Big Brother* – the world's first reality TV show – changed TV for ever. What happens when you put a group of young men and women in a house together and allow them no contact with the world outside? And what happens if they are on television twenty-four hours a day? A Dutchman called John De Mol had the original idea, and the first *Big Brother* appeared on TV in the Netherlands in 1999. More than twenty countries have had their own *Big Brothers* since then.

b Read the text again and complete the information below with a name or number.

1 The number of countries where *Baywatch* has appeared. <u>148</u>
2 The year *Baywatch* first appeared on TV. _____
3 The number of years it took to make *Walking with Dinosaurs*. _____
4 The number of countries where *Walking with Dinosaurs* has appeared. _____
5 The person who had the original idea for *Pop Idol*. _____
6 The winner of *Arab Super Star* in 2004. _____
7 The name of the most important character in *Fawlty Towers*. _____
8 When the last episode of *Fawlty Towers* appeared. _____
9 The person who had the original idea for *Big Brother*. _____
10 When *Big Brother* first appeared on Dutch TV. _____

Wordspot
feel

10 Complete the sentences with the correct form of *feel* and a word or phrase from the box.

about	cold	embarrassed	hot
like	~~like doing~~	sick	well

a What do you _feel like doing_ this weekend?

b Do you _____ something to eat before we go?

c This room _____ : who left the window open?

d Mum, come quickly! Sam says he _____ !

e I _____ so _____ when I broke Jose's glasses.

f How do you _____ Cara's plans to move overseas?

g Your head _____ . I think you've got a temperature.

h Joss went home because she didn't _____ very _____ .

Spelling
-ed endings

11 Look at the spelling rules on page 149 of the Students' Book and write the Past simple forms of these regular verbs.

a believe _____
b cry _____
c continue _____
d drop _____
e hurry _____
f use _____
g marry _____
h phone _____
i stop _____
j study _____

Pronunciation
Irregular verbs

12 a Which of the past verb forms in the box rhyme? Add them to the correct list.

~~came~~	fell	felt	gave	got	lost	met	paid	saw	sold
spoke	thought	told	was	wore					

made: _came_ _____ _____

went: _____ _____ _____

cost: _____ _____ _____

wrote: _____ _____ _____

bought: _____ _____ _____

b **T2.3** Listen and check. Repeat the verbs.

Improve your writing
Linkers: *but*, *so*, *because*, *then*

13 Correct the linkers to make the sentences logical.

a I'm really tired ___~~but~~___ *so* I'm going to bed.

b I couldn't buy anything ___~~so~~___ I forgot my purse.

c He's broken his arm ___~~because~~___ he can't play football.

d First you put in the cassette, ___~~but~~___ you press this button here.

e We got an expensive new computer this week, ___~~so~~___ we're having a lot of problems with it.

f The new teacher is very nice, ___~~then~~___ she's very strict about homework.

g It's terribly hot on the beach ___~~because~~___ we're taking the children home.

h His boss was angry with him ___~~so~~___ he was late for work three times in a week.

i Finish your drink: ___~~but~~___ we must go home.

MODULE 3

should/shouldn't

1 You are having dinner with people you don't know well. Which of the things below *should* you do and which *shouldn't* you do in your culture?

a You __*shouldn't*__ speak with your mouth full.

b You _____ wait for the others before you start eating.

c You _____ eat with your fingers.

d You _____ eat with your elbows on the table.

e You _____ make a noise when you drink something.

f You _____ put the knife in your mouth.

g You _____ use a spoon for soup.

h You _____ put your knife and fork on the plate when you finish.

can/can't

2 a Rewrite the sentences replacing the phrase in bold with *can* or *can't*.

1 **Is it possible** to borrow your dictionary?
   Can I borrow your dictionary?

2 My sister **is able to** speak three languages perfectly.
   _____

3 You **don't have permission to** come in here.
   _____

4 Now, **it is possible for you to** buy cheap plane tickets on the Internet.
   _____

5 **It's impossible for Renate to** come to the party.
   _____

6 **Are you able to** read French? I don't understand this.
   _____

7 '**We're not able to** answer the phone at the moment ...'
   _____

8 'Is it possible for us to sit by the window?'
   _____

b **T3.1** Listen and check. Practise saying the correct sentences.

have to / don't have to

3 Jodie is still at school. Her older brother, Ed, left school last month. Complete the conversation with *have to / don't have to* and a verb from the box.

| answer | be | do | find | ~~get up~~ | try | wear (x2) |
| worry (x2) | | write | | | | |

JODIE: You're so lucky Ed, you (a) _don't have to get up_ early every day and go to school.

ED: Yes, I know, but now I (b) _____ a job.

JODIE: That's not so bad – at least you (c) _____ homework every night.

ED: True, but I (d) _____ application letters and make lots of phone calls. It's boring!

JODIE: Not as boring as school – and you (e) _____ a horrible uniform.

ED: Well no, but I (f) _____ smart clothes when I go to a job interview.

JODIE: Hm, but you (g) _____ the teacher's questions all day ...

ED: What about the questions at the interview? I (h) _____ to answer those.

JODIE: OK, but you (i) _____ about exams.

ED: And you (j) _____ about earning money.

JODIE: Well, I (k) _____ good all week, so Mum and Dad give me my pocket money!

can/can't, have to / don't have to

4 Ben is going to take his driving test soon.
Complete the conversation with the correct form
of *have to* or *can*.

BEN: Is it true that there are two driving tests?

INSTRUCTOR: That's right: you (a) ___have to___ take a
written test and a practical – that's where
you're on the road with the examiner.

BEN: (b) _____ I take the practical test
first, please?

INSTRUCTOR: No, I'm sorry. You (c) _____ take
that test until you've passed the written
one.

BEN: Hm ... Is the written test very difficult?

INSTRUCTOR: No, not really. There are fifty questions, but
the good news is you (d) _____
answer all of them correctly. You
(e) _____ get 45 correct answers, so
you (f) _____ make a few mistakes
and still pass.

BEN: (g) _____ you give me some advice
about how to prepare for the written exam?

INSTRUCTOR: Learn all the rules of the road! But there are
thousands, so you (h) _____
remember everything at once – you
(i) _____ study a little bit every day.

BEN: OK. How about the practical exam?

INSTRUCTOR: Well, on the day, the examiner
(j) _____ see your driving licence.
Then he asks you to read a number plate to
check you (k) _____ see OK.

BEN: That sounds easy ... (l) _____
I take my test straight away?

INSTRUCTOR: Impossible! You (m) _____ learn to
park first – you won't pass if you
(n) _____ park your car!

Short answers with modal verbs *should, can, have to*

5 a When we answer questions with modal verbs,
we often use short answers, like this.

> LOOK!
>
> Should I / you / (s)he / it / we / they go?
> Yes, I / you / (s)he / it / we / they should.
> No, I / you / (s)he / it / we / they shouldn't.
>
> Can I / you / (s)he / it / we / they come?
> Yes, I / you / (s)he / it / we / they can.
> No, I / you / (s)he / it / we / they can't.
>
> Do I / you / we / they have to go?
> Yes, I / you / we / they do.
> No, I / you / we / they don't.
>
> Does (s)he / it have to go?
> Yes, (s)he / it does.
> No, (s)he / it doesn't.

b Complete the dialogues with short answers.

1 Can you and Jan come for a coffee after class?
No, we can't. I'm sorry – we have to go home.

2 Do I have to pay for the room now?
_____ . You can pay when you leave.

3 Should we phone to say we're going to be late?
_____ . Here's my phone.

4 Can we leave our coats here during the break?
_____ . But don't leave any money.

5 Do you think I should send a photograph with the
application form?
_____ . It's better if they can see what you
look like.

6 My son is six. Do I have to buy him a ticket?
_____ . It costs half the price of an adult
ticket.

7 Do you have to get up early tomorrow?
_____ . I can stay in bed!

8 Can you speak Japanese?
_____ . I lived there for ten years.

Vocabulary
Daily routine

6 a Complete the phrases with a word from the box.

about something	asleep	bed	dressed	of bed
off the alarm	shower	the alarm	the light	tired
to eat	up			

1	wake	_up_	7	switch	_____
2	fall	_____	8	get into	_____
3	get	_____	9	have something	_____
4	turn off	_____	10	feel	_____
5	set	_____	11	have a	_____
6	get out	_____	12	dream	_____

b Dave works at night, printing newspapers. Complete the text about his routine with a phrase from part a.

I started working nights two months ago, and it's a big change to my routine. Sometimes I'm so tired that I (1) _____ at work if there's nothing to do. I finish work at 5.30 a.m., go home, (2) _____ – it's quite dirty work – and (3) _____ at about 7a.m. I don't need to (4) _____ – it's light outside by then. I don't (5) _____ either, because I usually (6) _____ at around 1.30p.m. because of the noise of the school children playing outside. Often I still (7) _____ because I don't sleep well and I (8) _____ lots of strange things, like newspapers covering the sky and making it dark all the time! I finally (9) _____ at about 3 p.m: I (10) _____ (if I can find any clean clothes) and make a cup of coffee. I don't usually (11) _____ anything _____ , I'm not hungry until later.

Jobs

7 Use the clues to help you complete the names of the jobs from page 28 of the Students' Book.

a _f a r m e r_
b _ o _ _ _ _ _ _ _ _
c _ _ _ t _ _ _
d _ _ o _ _ _ _ _ _ _ _ _
e _ r _ _ _ _
f _ _ _ _ c _ _ _ _ _ _ _
g _ _ _ y _ _
h _ _ c _ _ _
i _ _ _ _ _ l _ _ _ _
j _ _ _ _ e
k _ _ c _ _ _ _ _ _
l _ _ _ _ _ o _ _ _ _ _ _
m _ _ u _ _ _ _
n _ _ r _ _
o _ _ _ _ _ i _ _ _ _ _
p _ _ _ _ e _ _ _ _ _ _
q _ _ r _ _ _

a works with animals
b writes for a newspaper
c looks after your teeth
d sells you things
e buys and sells things
f can arrest people
g you might need one if the police arrest you
h prepares food in a restaurant
i changes things into another language
j makes important decisions in a court of law
k designs houses and other buildings
l understands how people's minds work
m repairs things like water pipes in your house
n looks after people who are ill
o stops fires
p books your holiday
q serves drinks

Listen and read

8 **T3.2** Do you know the answers to these questions? Read and listen to the article *The Secrets of Sleep* and find the answers.

a How many hours a day do babies sleep?

_____

b How many hours should we sleep?

_____

c Give three reasons why it is bad for you to sleep for less than six hours a day.

_____

d How many hours do most people sleep?

_____

e Do older people need less sleep than younger people?

_____

f Does sleeping more than ten hours help you to wake up early the next day?

_____

The Secrets of Sleep

Babies do it for up to eighteen hours a day: Mrs Thatcher and Napoleon both said they only needed to do it three or four hours a night. Sleep. No one can live without it. But how much do we really need?

Research by the National Sleep Foundation in Washington says that we all need eight hours' sleep every night. Scientists have found that people who sleep for less than six and a half hours a night are more often ill than people who sleep for eight hours. Going without sleep also increases the chance of serious illness. 'Workaholics' who sleep for less than five hours often die young, and do less well at work.

The scientists found that, on average, adults sleep for seven hours a night, with thirty-two percent sleeping less than six hours. It also says that the idea that we need less sleep as we get older is completely untrue. 'People have no idea how important sleep is to their lives,' Dr Thomas Roth, director of the Foundation says. 'Good health needs good sleep.'

'But not too much of it,' says Professor Jim Horne of Loughborough University. 'Sleep is like food and drink,' he believes: 'you would always like to have a little bit more, but that doesn't mean you need it.' Professor Horne studied a group of people who could spend as many hours as they wanted in bed; after ten hours they didn't find it any easier to get up in the morning. And people who sleep for more than nine hours a night die younger than people who usually sleep for seven or eight!

Adapted from The Week *4 April 1998 & 30 May 1998.*

Real life
Making requests and asking for permission

9 Put the words in the correct order to make sentences then write them in the correct space below.

a have / I / water / of / Can / glass / a

b I / call / OK / it / make / if / Is / phone / a

c say / again / you / that / Could / please

d moment / Can / you / for / I / speak / a / to

e mind / CDs / look / Do / at / you / I / your / if

f if / lesson / OK / miss / Is / English / it / tomorrow / I / the

g you / over / Could / please / move

h turn / Do / I / the / up / mind / TV / if / you

1 A: _____ ?
   B: Yes of course, what about?

2 A: _____ ?
   I didn't understand.
   B: Oh sorry, I said we only have £50 tickets left.

3 A: _____ ?
   B: Well, all right. If it's a local call.

4 A: _____ ?
   I can't hear it.
   B: Oh sure – the remote's on the table.

5 A: _____ ?
   B: Well, not really. Why can't you come?

6 A: _____ ?
   I'm really thirsty.
   B: Of course – there's a bottle in the fridge.

7 A: _____ ?
   B: Go ahead. You can borrow some if you want.

8 A: _____ ?
   B: Yes, sorry, I didn't realise you wanted to sit down.

Vocabulary booster: studying

10 **a** Label the pictures with phrases from the box.

fail an exam   get a certificate   get lots of homework   graduate learn something by heart   pass an exam   research an assignment on the Internet revise for an exam   take a course   take an exam

1 _____

2 _____

3 _____

4 _____

5 _____

6 _____

7 _____

8 _____

9 _____

10 _____

b **T3.3** Listen and check. Practise saying the words.

c Put the phrases in part a into the table below.

People usually like to do this	People don't usually like to do this	It depends
pass an exam		

Pronunciation
The letter 'a'

11 a **T3.4** There are a number of different ways to pronounce the letter 'a'. Listen:

/æ/ e.g.: have to	/ɑː/ e.g.: can't	/eɪ/ e.g.: make

b Here are some other words from module 3. Put the underlined letter 'a' in the correct column according to its pronunciation.

acrobat   alarm   architect   barman   catch
dangerous   farmer   fast   game   graduate
patient   snack   stay   taxi   wake up

c **T3.5** Listen and check. Practise saying the words.

Improve your writing
Writing a paragraph

12 1 Read the sentences below and put them into the correct order.

a   That's why I think that everyone should learn at least one foreign language from the age of eight.

b   Also, children are less worried about making mistakes when they learn than adults.

c   Nowadays, communication between people from different countries is more important than ever before.

d   The main reason for this is that many people say it gets harder to learn a new language as you get older.

1 _____   2 _____   3 _____

4 _____

2 Which sentence:

a   introduces the topic?   _____

b   gives the writer's opinion?   _____

c   gives a reason?   _____

d   gives another reason?   _____

3 Write a similar paragraph yourself about one of the topics below. Use the language in the box to help you.

- the school-leaving age
- military service
- going to university
- learning to drive a car
- learning to use a computer

Nowadays, ... is more important than ever before,
That's why I think that ...
I think that everyone should ...
The main reason for this is that ...
Also ...

Spelling
Finding mistakes

13 Read the paragraph about Stefan below. There is a total of ten spelling mistakes. Find and correct the mistakes.

between
Stefan has a 'gap year' ~~bitween~~ finishing school and starting his university corse in engineering. Diferent people give him advise about the best thing to do for that year. His pearents think he should get a job and ern lots of money. His teacher suggests volantary work and tells him not to wurry about money. His girlfreind wants him to work with her, and his best friend says he should teach English somewere sunny, like him.

MODULE 4

Present continuous

1 Put the verb in brackets into the correct form of the Present continuous: positive, negative, question or short answer.

a A: Good evening.
   Are you enjoying
   (you / enjoy) yourselves?

   B: Oh, yes! _We're having_
   (we / have) a fantastic time, thank you!

b A: I'm sorry, _____
   (I / drive) too fast for you?

   B: Yes, _____ .
   Could you slow down a bit?

c A: What _____
   (you / do)?

   B: There's a film on TV, but _____
   (I / not / watch) it really.

d A: What's the problem?

   B: _____ (look for) my keys. _____
   (you / sit) on them?

   A: Oh, yes, here they are, sorry!

e It's Sunday, so Virginia _____ (not / work) today. She _____
   (spend) some time at home for a change.

f A: Where _____
   (you / go)?

   B: Shopping. Do you want to come?

   A: I can't. My parents _____ (wait) for me.

State and action verbs

LOOK!

Some verbs describe things which stay the same. These are called **state** verbs. We don't usually use them in the continuous form.
Verbs of feeling: *like, love, hate*
Verbs of thinking: *believe, know, understand*

Other verbs describe things that can happen quickly. These are called **action** verbs. We can use them either in simple or continuous forms.
*He's **driving** home.*
*He **drives** home every day.*

2 Tick (✓) the sentences which are correct. Put a cross (✗) by the sentences which are wrong, and correct them.

a Are you liking coffee? ✗ _Do you like coffee?_

b Do you like coffee? ✓ _____

c I'm not believing you! _____

d Do you want a drink? _____

e I'm not understanding him. _____

f I'm hating cold weather! _____

g I don't understand Turkish. _____

h I'm not knowing her name. _____

Present simple or Present continuous?

3 Circle the correct form: Present simple or Present continuous.

a A: What languages *are you speaking /*(*do you speak*)?

   B: English, French and Italian.

b A: [BANG] Ow!

   B: What's the matter – what *do you do / are you doing*?

c A: What's that song *you listen to / you're listening to*?

   B: It's called 'Angels'. Good, isn't it?

d A: What *are you reading / do you read*?

   B: It's an article about holidays in Switzerland.

e A: *Do you smoke / Are you smoking*?

   B: No, thank you. I stopped smoking two years ago.

f A: Why *are you laughing / do you laugh*?

   B: It's your face. You look so funny!

g A: *Does your brother play / Is your brother playing* any sport?

   B: Yes. Football in the winter, tennis in the summer and swimming all year.

h A: Paul. PAUL! *Are you listening / Do you listen* to me?

   B: Hm? What? Sorry?

Present continuous for future arrangements

4 **a** Look at the family calendar for next week. Write sentences about the four family members, like this:
Steve isn't working on Monday. He's playing squash with Andy at 10.30.

_____
_____
_____
_____
_____
_____
_____
_____
_____
_____
_____
_____
_____
_____
_____
_____
_____

	Steve	Judy	Oliver	Florence
Mon 7	No work! Squash with Andy 10.30	work		swimming
Tues 8	to Manchester for the day. Train at 06.45	doctor's at 09.15	football at 16.00	
Wed 9		work	to Tom's house after school	
Thurs 10	cinema with Jan and Chris (Steve's mum to babysit)			
Fri 11		meet Alison for lunch - 13.00	meeting cousins in the park at 14.30	
Sat 12				
Sun 13	lunch with grandparents at 12.00			

b T4.1 Practise saying the sentences.

5 Put the words in the correct order to make questions and write answers that are true for you.

a going / you / Where / your / are / this / holidays / year / for

_____
_____
_____ ?

b you / week / a / having / Are / this / off / day

_____
_____
_____ ?

c next / you / doing / What / weekend / are

_____
_____
_____ ?

d future / to / relatives / visit / coming / Are / near / your / in / the

_____
_____
_____ ?

e are / lesson / English / When / next / having / you / your

_____
_____
_____ ?

f meeting / today / you / friends / later / Are / your

_____
_____
_____ ?

g dinner / in / evening / Who's / your / cooking / house / this

_____
_____
_____ ?

h anyone / the / month / Is / this / dentist / your / going / family / in / to

_____
_____
_____ ?

Vocabulary
Special occasions

6 Choose the correct word from the box to complete the sentences.

~~dress~~	have	stay	buy	visit	send	eat
make	invited	cooked	exchange			

a At the Carnival, many people _____ _dress_ _____ up in colourful clothes.

b It was your cousin's birthday yesterday. Did you remember to _____ her a card?

c During the week, I have to be at home by eleven, but at the weekend I can _____ up late.

d People in Britain often _____ relatives on Christmas Day. After lunch, they often _____ presents.

e At the end of the course, our teacher _____ everyone in the class to her house for dinner.

f I don't feel well today. I'm going to _____ the day off work.

g It's Valentine's Day tomorrow so don't forget to _____ some flowers for your wife!

h Charlie's mum is going to _____ a special cake for his birthday.

i I haven't go enough money to _____ out at the moment: Christmas was very expensive!

j When I passed all my exams, my mum _____ me a special meal.

Real life
Phrases for special occasions

7 In the dialogues below, tick (✓) the phrases that are correct, and change any that are not.

a A: Julia's twenty-one today, Oliver.
   B: Happy anniversary, Julia.

b A: I can't come in to work today, I've got the 'flu.
   B: Oh well, good health!

c A: We've just been to the hospital – we're going to have a baby.
   B: Congratulations!

d A: Turn the music down, it's midnight.
   B: Merry New Year, everybody!

e A: I brought you these flowers – shall I put them by your bed?
   B: Thank you very much, it's lovely.

f A: Thank you for coming.
   B: Thank you for inviting us: it was a lovely ceremony.

g A: It's our fortieth wedding anniversary today.
   B: Really? Many happy returns!

h A: Well, goodbye, and the good luck for the future.
   B: Thank you for teaching me, I really enjoyed your lessons.

Wordspot
day

8 a Complete the sentences with a word/words from the box.

~~after tomorrow~~	all	bad	before yesterday
every	off	one	out for the	seven	the other
twice			

1 The day _after tomorrow_ is Sunday.

2 I clean my teeth _____ a day, _____ days a week.

3 I hope I'll be famous _____ day.

4 I do some exercise _____ day.

5 I had a _____ day yesterday.

6 The day _____ was Wednesday.

7 I'm going _____ day on Saturday.

8 I stayed at home _____ day yesterday.

9 I saw a good film _____ day.

10 I don't often have a day _____ .

b Change the sentences where necessary so that they are true for you.

Vocabulary booster: special occasions

9 **a** Look at the pictures and label the numbered items with the correct word from the box.

> presents   paper plates   candles   someone blowing out candles   glasses
> the host and hostess   birthday cake   guests   decorations   paper cups
> sandwiches   cards

1 ___

2 ___

3 ___

4 ___

5 ___

6 ___

7 ___

8 ___

9 ___

10 ___

11 ___

12 ___

b **T4.2** Listen and practise saying the words.

Religious festivals around the world

Islamic festivals – Ramadan

Because the Islamic religion uses a calendar based on the moon, not the sun, the exact date of religious festivals changes from year to year. The Islamic calendar begins with the *hijra*, the year when Mohammed left the city of Mecca for Medina. The New Year is a time for peaceful prayer for most Muslim people. Every year, in the month of Ramadan – the ninth month of the Islamic calendar – all Muslims <u>fast</u> from early morning until evening.

By living without everyday comforts, even for a short time, a fasting person better understands the life of poor people who are hungry, and also grows in his or her spiritual life.

Easter in Poland

In Poland, there are many customs at Easter: for example, the 'blessing basket', containing (among other things) coloured eggs, bread, salt and white sausages. Everything in the basket has a meaning: the eggs represent Christ, the bread, salt and sausages good health and enough money in the coming year. The family Easter breakfast on Sunday morning is as important as Christmas dinner for Poles. And there is one more Polish tradition connected with Easter Monday: 'watering'. People throw water at each other, and this is a wish for good health, too. Even strangers on the street are not safe from a bath of cold water on Easter Monday!

A Hindu festival – Diwali

The festival of Diwali is one of the most important religious festivals in India. It lasts for five days around the end of October. It is the festival of Laxmi, the Goddess who, in the Hindu religion, brings peace and prosperity.

Preparations for the festival begin several weeks before the festival itself. People clean and decorate their homes, prepare special food and buy new clothes and jewellery to welcome the Goddess into their homes. All over India, people light up their homes with oil lamps and colourful lights.

The celebrations take place on the darkest night of the lunar month, Amavasya. In the evening, fireworks fill the sky to make Diwali a true 'Festival of Light'.

Glossary
fast = to eat no food or drink

Listen and read

10 a **T4.3** Read and listen to the texts on the opposite page about three different religious festivals. In which festival do people:
1 clean and decorate their homes?
2 throw water at people in the street?
3 try to understand the problems of the poor?
4 have a special basket of food?
5 not eat between morning and evening?
6 buy new clothes?
7 put bright lights in their homes?

b Read again and listen to the texts. Answer these questions.
1 Are Islamic festivals at the same time each year?
2 Which month is Ramadan?
3 What does the 'blessing basket' contain?
4 Which meal is very important to Poles at Easter?
5 In which country is Diwali celebrated?
6 How long is the festival of Diwali?
7 Which Goddess is it the festival of?

Improve your writing
A letter of invitation

11 Write out the letter below with capital letters and correct punctuation.

10 fife road
norton

7th october

dear tony

sorry i haven't written for so long but i've been really busy with the new job I hope you're well and still enjoying life at university
the main reason i'm writing is to tell you that valerie and I are staying at uncle frank's villa in spain for the Easter holidays would you like to come and stay for a few days the villa is in a really beautiful place very near the beach you can fly to malaga airport and get a bus from there
can you give me a ring to tell me if you're interested our new phone number is 01804 742 3812 we'd love to see you
see you soon

mark

Spelling
-ing forms

12 Look at the spelling rules on page 150 of the Students' Book. Tick (✓) the correct spellings and correct the ones that are wrong.

celebrateing ✗   _celebrating_
cooking   _____
driveing   _____
getting   _____
giveing   _____
inviteing   _____
liveing   _____
putting   _____
studying   _____
taking   _____
writeing   _____
visitting   _____

Pronunciation
/ð/ and /θ/

13 a **T4.4** Listen to the underlined sounds in these words and phrases from module 4 and put them in the correct column: /ð/ or /θ/.

Mo<u>th</u>er's Day   Fa<u>th</u>er's Day   bir<u>th</u>day
twenty-fif<u>th</u>   four<u>th</u>   <u>th</u>irty-first   <u>th</u>e o<u>th</u>er day
<u>th</u>e day before yesterday   nei<u>th</u>er of us
to ge<u>th</u>er   your good heal<u>th</u>   <u>Th</u>anks for coming!

/ð/	/θ/
Mother's Day	_____
_____	_____
_____	_____
_____	_____
_____	_____
_____	

b Listen again and practise saying the words.

Comparative and superlative adjectives

Comparative forms

1 a Read the profiles of Paul Chang and Mike 'The Monster' Morton. Use the adjectives in brackets to complete the questions and answers below.

	PAUL CHANG	MIKE 'THE MONSTER' MORTON
Age:	19	36
Height:	1.85m	1.78m
Strength:	Very fast	Slow
Weakness:	Not very experienced	Very experienced
Weight:	80kg	95kg
Aggression factor:	80%	95%
Power rating:	7/10	9/10
Popularity	☺ ☺ ☺	☺

Who is ...

1 (old)   *older?*
             Mike is older than Paul.

2 (young)   _____ ?
             _____

3 (tall)   _____ ?
             _____

4 (fast)   _____ ?
             _____

5 (experienced) _____ ?
             _____

6 (slow)   _____ ?
             _____

7 (heavy)   _____ ?
             _____

8 (aggressive) _____ ?
             _____

9 (powerful) _____ ?
             _____

10 (popular) _____ ?
             _____

b **15.1** Listen and practise saying the sentences.

Superlative forms

2 Put the adjectives into the superlative form.

a The _____*tallest*_____ (tall) US President was Abraham Lincoln, who was 1m 93, and the _____ (old) was Ronald Reagan, who was 69 when he became President in 1981.

b The _____ (fast) winner of a London Marathon was the Portuguese runner Antonio Pinto – fourteen minutes better than the _____ (quick) woman, Ingrid Kristiansen from Norway.

c Sultan Hassanal Bolkiah, Sultan of the Arab state of Brunei, is the world's _____ (rich) monarch. Many people think that Queen Elizabeth of Great Britain is the _____ (wealthy) female ruler.

d Elvis Presley – who died in 1977– was probably the _____ (popular) singer of all time. He always said that the _____ (important) person in his life was his mother.

e Queen Jane had the _____ (short) time on the throne of any English Queen – just five days! King Louis XIV of France was King for the _____ (long) time: seventy-two years!

3 〔T5.2〕 Here are some famous sayings which contain a comparative or superlative adjective. Listen to the sayings and underline the comparative and superlative forms.

a

> Democracy is the <u>worst</u> form of government … apart from all the others.

Winston Churchill

b

> The reason I wanted to be an actress was to play people much more interesting than I am, and to say things much more intelligent than anything I could think of myself.

Actress Prunella Scales

c

> All animals are equal, but some are more equal than others.

George Orwell in Animal Farm

d

> Good, better, the best
> Never let it rest
> Until good is better
> And better is the best

Unknown teacher

e

> **Being funny is much more difficult than being clever.**

Editor of a comedy magazine

Prepositions in comparative phrases: *as, than, from, like, in, to*

4 Complete the sentences with *as, than, from, like, in* or *to*.

a Marie's dress is very similar ___*to*___ mine.

b She has the same taste in clothes _____ me.

c Anna is older _____ she looks.

d Helen is the tallest person _____ our class.

e Do you look _____ your parents?

f Who's the youngest person _____ your family?

g Our lives today are very different _____ the way our grandparents lived.

h Are these glasses the same _____ yours?

Making comparisons with nouns

5 Circle the correct form in the sentences.

> We compare nouns using *more* and *the most.*
> *You've got **more** CDs than me.*
> *My brother has **the most** CDs in our family.*

a My dog's got a lot (more) / *the most* energy than me!

b Sylvia wears *more / the most* jewellery in the class.

c All my friends spend *more / the most* money on clothes than me.

d There are *more / the most* books on the floor than on the bookshelves.

e Radio FM123 plays *more / the most* rock music of all the stations.

f Who has *more / the most* brothers and sisters: Alice or Fatima?

g Your team lost *more / the most* games than mine.

h Which person in your class watched *more / the most* TV programmes last night?

Describing people
Questions about appearance

6 a Write the questions for these answers about Donna.

1 ___*How old is she?*_____
She's in her twenties.

2 _____ ?
She's slim and athletic-looking.

3 _____ ?
About 1m 75.

4 _____ ?
She's very friendly.

5 _____ ?
No, it's quite long.

6 _____ ?
They're dark brown.

b 〔T5.3〕 Listen and check. Then listen and repeat.

31

is or *has got*?

7 Complete the sentences with *is* ('s) / *are* or *has* ('s) / *have* ('ve) *got*.

a   My grandmother _____*is*_____ in her seventies, but she _____ a very young face. She _____ lovely teeth and skin and she _____ (not) any white hair!

b   My brothers and sisters _____ very similar to look at – they _____ all very pale and they _____ green eyes and red hair.

c   The baby _____ only a few days old, but she _____ lots and lots of hair.

d   My dad _____ a moustache, but he (not) _____ a beard any more – he shaved it off a few weeks ago!

That's him!

8 Complete the conversation with words or phrases from the box.

younger than	looked	Did he have
Taller than	~~What did he~~	he's got
elegant	what colour was	the strangest
have a look	similar to	clean-shaven

MO = Mrs Ogden   PO = Police Officer

PO: So, tell me about the man who stole your neighbours' car.

(a) _*What did he*_ look like?

MO: Well, he was tall …

PO: (b) _____ me?

MO: Oh yes, and he was (c) _____ you – only about thirty, I'd say.

PO: Humph! And (d) _____ his hair?

MO: It was blond, and short … it was (e) _____ yours, actually.

PO: I see. (f) _____ a beard?

MO: No, he was (g) _____ .

PO: OK. Now (h) _____ at these photos – can you see him?

MO: Oh yes, he (i) _____ exactly like this one here.

PO: But that's Frankie 'Fingers' Farnham – (j) _____ a beard, and he's very short! Do you remember anything else about the man?

MO: Yes, (k) _____ thing was that he was very (l) _____ – he was wearing a suit … not like a thief at all.

PO: Hm, like this photo?

MO: Yes, that's him!

PO: That's Bill 'the Businessman' Mahony: he's in prison! Are you sure you saw the thief?

MO: Well, er, it was very dark …

Order of adjectives

LOOK!

> When we use more than one adjective before a noun, the order is:
>
> | size | shape | colour | noun |
> |------|-------|--------|------|
> | long | | dark | hair |
> | big | square | | glasses |
>
> | opinion | other adjectives | noun |
> |---------|------------------|------|
> | a pretty | young | woman |
>
> We do **not** use *and*:
> She's got long ~~and~~ dark hair.

9 Tick (✓) the sentence if the word order is correct. Put a cross (✗) if the word order is wrong, and correct it.

a   Sue's little daughter's got ~~blue big~~ *big blue* eyes and ~~blond long~~ *long blonde* hair.

b   Kerry wore a very elegant, long, black dress to the theatre.

c   Harry's got a grey short beard and a moustache.

d   I saw some silver gorgeous earrings when I was shopping today.

e   You know Jon – he's got short dark hair and he wears small round glasses

f   I always wear old casual clothes at home.

g   Cindy's tall, and she's got pale beautiful skin.

h   We saw a strange-looking old man waiting at the bus stop.

Vocabulary
Adjectives to describe appearance

10 Cross out the word that does **not** belong in each group.

a	pretty	attractive	ugly	good-looking
b	blond	dark-haired	dyed	long
c	enormous	young	old	in her twenties
d	pale	fair-skinned	tanned	clean-shaven
e	elegant	sophisticated	polite	casual

Physical appearance

11 Use the clues to complete the grid below. The words all come from pages 42–43 of the Students' Book.

a   Eighteenth-century ladies – and men – often wore a _____ on their head. (3 letters)

b   Physically strong and good at sport. (8 letters)

c   You are this if you have a lot of courage. (5 letters)

d   When your skin goes brown because of the sun, you have one of these. (6 letters)

e   In the times of Queen Elizabeth I, fashionable ladies wanted their faces to be this colour! (5)

f   If you eat something which is _____ , you will be very ill. (9 letters)

g   The opposite of blond is *dark-* (6 letters)

h   It's between your head and your shoulders! (4 letters)

i   For skin colour, the opposite of dark. (4 letters)

j   Thin, in an attractive way. (4 letters)

k   People put this on their face to look more attractive. (4 letters, 2 letters)

l   People put this liquid on their skin: it has a pleasant smell. (7 letters)

a W I G
b H
c A
d T
e I
f S
g H
h E
i L
j I
k K
l E
   ?

Vocabulary booster: parts of the face and body

12 a Label the pictures.

1

2

3

4

5

6

7

8

9

10

11

12

13

14

15

16

17

18

b **T5.4** Listen and practise the pronunciation of the words.

c How many does a person usually have? Write the words from part a next to the correct number below.

1: _head_ , _____ , _____ , _____ , _____ , _____ ,

_____

2: _____ , _____ , _____ , _____ , _____ , _____ ,

_____

10: _____ , _____

32: _____

Uncountable: _____

Wordspot
look

13 Use an expression from the box to complete these sentences.

| looking forward   look for   look at   look up |
| look like   Look out   ~~looking~~   look after |
| looks good |

a He was a very good *looking* _____ man, but he wasn't very intelligent.

b Could you help me _____ my bag? I can't find it anywhere.

c I hope Mandy doesn't ask me to _____ her children today.

d I'm really _____ to my summer holidays – we're going to visit my cousin in Rio.

e Tim _____ really _____ in that suit, doesn't he?

f _____ ! There's something in the middle of the road.

g You could _____ the phone number on the Internet if you're not sure.

h He loves to _____ himself in the mirror.

Pronunciation
The letter 'o'

14 a **T5.5** There are a number of different ways to pronounce the letter 'o'. Listen:

/ɔː/ e.g.: **more**	/əʊ/ e.g.: **most**	/ɒ/ e.g.: **got**

b **T5.6** Listen to the pronunciation of the words below. In each pair, is the sound in bold the same or different? Practise saying the words.

1	both	important	*different*
2	old	slow	*the same*
3	morning	dog	_____
4	toe	nose	_____
5	modern	photograph	_____
6	popular	organised	_____
7	local	strong	_____
8	sport	**your**	_____

Improve your writing
Writing a description

15 a Read the description a student wrote of someone in her family. Which sentence talks about:

1 who the person is, and the writer's relationship to her? _____ E _____

2 her general appearance? _____

3 her build and height? _____

4 her eyes? _____

5 her hair? _____

6 her age? _____

A She's a very attractive little girl – she always looks happy and she's got a lovely smile.

B Her eyes are blue, just like her father's.

C She's about average height for her age ... and she's quite slim.

D She's got beautiful, blonde hair ... and it's her natural colour!

E Louise is my youngest cousin, and she lives not far from my family.

F She'll be ten next birthday.

b Make some notes about someone you know well, or someone in your family. Write a paragraph using the suggested order in part a.

Useful phrases
X is my ... , and (s)he lives ...
(S)he's a very ... man/woman/girl/boy and (s)he's got a lovely ...
(S)he's got ... hair/eyes.
His/Her eyes are ... / and (s)he's got long/short, dark/blond hair.
(S)he's about ... tall / about average height.
(S)he's ... years old / (S)he'll be ... next birthday.

Intentions and wishes: *going to*, *planning to*, *would like to*, *would rather*
Positive and negative forms

1 Write sentences about the Craven family.

a   Rob and Sofia Craven live in England but they / plan / move / to California.

Rob and Sofia Craven live in England but they are planning to move to California.

b   Rob is a cameraman and he / going / work / in a film studio there.

_____

_____

c   Sofia is a music teacher, but she / not / plan / work / for the first few months.

_____

_____

d   They / going / sell / their car, but they / not / going / sell their house. A friend of theirs / going / rent / it.

_____

_____

e   The children / plan / take / their dog with them, but Rob and Sofia / plan / leave / him in England. They / going / buy / another dog in California.

_____

_____

f   In California, Sofia / like / buy / a house by the beach, but Rob / rather / have / an apartment with a big garden. The children / like / live / next door to Cameron Diaz!

_____

_____

g   Emily says she / like / have a horse, but Todd / rather / get / another dog.

_____

_____

h   Emily / like / learn / to ride, but Todd / rather / learn / to surf.

_____

_____

Question forms

2 Here are some answers about the Craven family. Write the questions.

a   <u>Where are they planning</u>
    <u>to move?</u>
    To California.

b   _____
    _____ ?
    In a film studio.

c   _____
    _____ ?
    No, not for the first few months.

d   _____
    _____ ?
    Yes they are, but not their house.

e   _____
    _____ ?
    A friend of theirs.

f   _____
    _____ ?
    No, they're planning to leave him in England.

g   _____
    _____ ?
    No, he'd rather have a big garden.

h   _____
    _____ ?
    Next door to Cameron Diaz.

i   _____
    _____ ?
    A horse.

j   _____
    _____ ?
    He'd rather learn to surf.

3 Read the newspaper column. Choose the phrases from the box to fill the gaps.

~~going to~~   he's   I would   planning to   not planning
I'm planning   is going   to retire   rather

Seen and heard

The best of this week's celebrity gossip

by **Stella Renuzzi**

Glamorous actress, Sophie de Roy, has said that she is in love with Argentinian dancer Hector Castagni. 'He's the perfect man for me,' she told me, 'It's not easy being a single girl, but I hope that's (a) _goîng to_ change soon.' 'Sophie and I are both very young,' said Castagni in an interview with KO magazine. 'I would (b) _____ wait for a few years before we make any important decisions. I'm (c) _____ to get married till I'm thirty.'

Ex-footballer Jim Norton is in Hollywood hoping for a career in films. And the good news for Jim is that he has found his first film role – (d) _____ going to play the part of 'Badger' – a violent criminal – in the new Mo Amos film, *Gun Runner*. 'I don't think there's a big difference between acting and playing football,' he said to me, 'so I'm (e) _____ move here to help my film career.'

Angry that his last film *Smash!!* did not win the Academy Award, film director Donald Braine has said that he's going (f) _____ from show business. 'If no one likes my films, that's not my problem,' he said. 'The film world is not important to me. I'm more interested in my new restaurant (also called *Smash!!*).' And he has more news: '(g) _____ to open another restaurant (*Smash!! 2*) in Los Angeles next year,' he says.

Holly Pratelli – star of the TV Soap Opera *Hope Street* – (h) _____ to leave the series. She says it's because she doesn't like her new co-star, Chuck Ryder. 'I don't think he's handsome at all,' she told me. 'One day, (i) _____ like to have a big romantic scene with British actor Roy Thinn – he's gorgeous!'

Glossary

gossip = conversation or writing about other people's behaviour and private lives

Predictions

will and *won't*

4 Put *will* or *won't* in the best place in the sentences.

a It _won't_ be difficult to find accommodation – there aren't many tourists at this time of year.

b Do you think we be able to buy tickets when we get there?

c I'm sorry, but there be any time for us to have lunch.

d You be all right if I go out for a couple of hours?

e I'm going to Michelle's party on Sunday. You be there too?

f Don't worry. I'm sure there be any problems getting a visa.

g How long it take for us to get there?

h There be any food at your party?

Short answers with *will*, *won't* and *going to*

> Will you / (s)he / it / we / they be here tomorrow?
>   Yes, I / (s)he / it / we / they will.
>   No, I / (s)he / it / we / they won't.
> Are you / we / they going to be there?
>   Yes, I am.
>   Yes, we / you / they are.
>   No, I'm not.
>   No, we're / you're / they're not.
> Is (s)he / it going to be there?
>   Yes, (s)he / it is.
>   No, (s)he / it isn't.

LOOK!

5 Write in the correct short answer.

a Will Antonella be at the party on Friday?   Yes, *she will.*

b Are you going to say sorry?   No, _____

c Is it going to be a nice day?   Yes, _____

d Will you be at home if I phone you at ten?   No, _____

e Are Jill and Rory going to come with us?   No, _____

f Are you going to see Frank this afternoon?   Yes, _____

g Will it take a long time to get to the airport?   No, _____

h Will you be here next month?   Yes, _____

Pronunciation
'll, *will* and *won't*

6   a   **T6.1**   Listen to how we pronounce *'ll*, *will* and *won't*.

'll: I'll go, I'll see, It'll be, There'll be
will: Will you see …? Will there be …? Will it be …? Yes, I will, Yes there will
won't: I won't stay, It won't happen, They won't go, There won't be time

b   **T6.2**   Listen and complete the sentences. Then listen and repeat.

1   ____*I'll*____ see you after my holiday.
2   _____ have a great time!
3   _____ be at home tomorrow.
4   _____ be at home later?
5   Yes, _____ .
6   _____ be crowded?
7   No, _____ .
8   _____ be here soon.
9   _____ be time to go to the zoo?
10   No, _____ .

Real life
Social chit-chat

7   a Match the beginnings of the questions in A with the endings in B.

A	B
1 Is he feeling	on holiday?
2 Horrible day,	time in Madrid?
3 Did you have a	for the weekend?
4 Did you get	to be back?
5 Have you got any plans	good weekend? nice weather?
6 Is it your first	better now?
7 Are you glad	isn't it?
8 Are you here	

b   Write the questions from part a in the correct place.

1   *Have you got any plans for the weekend* ?
Yes, we're going to visit my aunt and uncle.

2   _____
_____ ?
It was very busy. I had friends for lunch on Sunday.

3   _____
_____ ?
Terrible. I hate the rain!

4   _____
_____ ?
No, actually I'm working here for a few days.

5   How's your little boy?
_____ ?
Oh yes, he's going back to school tomorrow.

6   How was the holiday?
_____ ?
Beautiful. It was lovely and warm every day.

7   _____ ?
Not really. I've got so much to do at work now.

8   _____ ?
No, I came here once when I was only ten – I don't remember much.

Vocabulary
Holidays

8 a Choose a word from the box to match one of the definitions below.

a cruise	a nightmare	an excursion	crowded
delayed	luxurious	nightlife	peaceful
polluted	self-catering	tasty	~~warm~~

1 between hot and cold ___*warm*___

2 comfortable, beautiful and expensive _____

3 damaged by gases or chemicals _____

4 a holiday on a large ship _____

5 good to eat or drink _____

6 entertainment in the evening _____

7 you cook your own food _____

8 too full of people or things _____

9 calm and quiet _____

10 a short journey to visit a place _____

11 late because of something like bad weather or traffic _____

12 a bad experience or a bad dream _____

b Complete the sentences with a word from the box in part a.

1 When we visited Japan, we had a dish called *teriyaki* which was very ___*tasty*___ .

2 At the weekend, the beach got so _____ , there was nowhere for us to sit.

3 Let's have a swim! The water's quite _____ .

4 Have you booked _____ today? I'm going to visit the castle.

5 Your flight is _____ by about two hours.

6 Unfortunately, the lake near the industrial plant is now so _____ that all the fish have died.

7 We stayed in a cabin in the mountains, far from any roads or towns. It was very _____ .

8 I hope the _____ is good in this place. I'd really like to go dancing.

9 I hate _____ holidays: I want someone else to do the cooking for a change!

10 The Hotel Metropole is a five-star hotel; one of the most _____ hotels in the city.

11 We're planning to go on _____ round the Mediterranean next year.

12 My handbag was stolen at the airport, and then I missed my flight – what a _____ !

Vocabulary booster: things you take on holiday

9 a Dave is going on holiday. Look at the picture and tick (✓) the items in the box that he has remembered to pack. What has he forgotten?

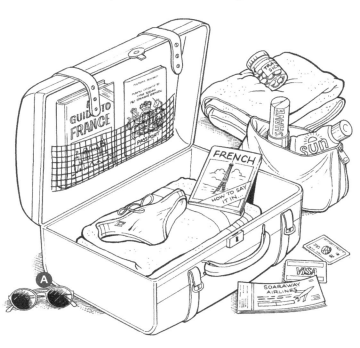

passport	sun cream	sunglasses	guide book
swimming trunks	shaving foam	phrase book	
towels	credit cards	plane tickets	toothbrush
travel sickness pills			

b **T6.3** Listen and practise saying the words.

c Put the words into one of the columns below.

Things you need during a journey	Things you need for the beach	Things you need in a strange town	Other
passport	*sun cream*		

Listen and read

10 **10.4** Read and listen to the information about holiday offers. Find the answers to the questions below:

a Which is the cheapest holiday destination?

_____

b If you want information about cheap flights to Hong Kong, what number should you phone?

_____

c How long is the holiday in Sorrento?

_____

d Which hotel do you stay at in Boston?

_____

e How much does the holiday in Spain cost?

_____

f On what date does the holiday in Syria begin?

_____

g Can you buy a cheap ticket to Sorrento after March 31?

_____

h Where do you learn salsa dancing?

_____

i What is the shortest time you can stay in Hong Kong?

_____

j What's the price of the trip to Lille?

_____

k Which holiday is cheaper for children?

_____

l How many days does the tour of Syria last?

_____

A **Dance and ski in Spain**
Dance Holidays (01206 5777000) is offering a seven-day holiday combining skiing in the Sierra Nevada and salsa dancing in Granada. The price, £395, includes flights, <u>B&B</u> and ski pass.

B **Eurostar to Lille**
Time Off (0870 584 6363) has two nights at the Grand Hotel Bellevue in Lille for £179. This price includes return Eurostar tickets, accommodation and breakfast.

C *Bargain flights to Hong Kong*
Trailfinders (020 7938 3366) has cut-price fares to Hong Kong for only £310 on KLM. Departures are from Stansted Airport until 10 April. The minimum stay required is seven days, the maximum is one month.

D *Bargain in Boston*
Virgin Holidays (01293 456789) has three nights at the two-star Midtown Hotel in Boston for £299 until 28 March. Flights depart from Gatwick and children under 11 pay half price.

E *Tour of Syria*
The Imaginative Traveller (020 8742 8612) has a nine-day tour of Syria. The trip, which includes Palmyra and Damascus, leaves on 24 March and costs £695, with flights, hotels and guides.

F *Week in Sorrento*
Citalia *(020 8686 5533) has seven nights in Sorrento for £399. This includes* <u>half-board</u> *accommodation in the Hotel Bristol and flights. The offer applies to departures on 31 March.*

Glossary
B&B = the hotel price includes bed and breakfast   *half-board* = the hotel price includes bed, breakfast and dinner

Improve your writing
More postcards

11 **a** Read the three postcards below. In each case, find out:

1 who sent the postcard, and from where.

A _____

B _____

C _____

2 the relationship between the sender and the receiver.

A _____

B _____

C _____

3 is the sender enjoying her/himself?

A _____ B _____ C _____

Hi everyone!
I can't believe we're finally in Bangkok,
it's fantastic, very hot and crowded (a bit like the
office really ...), lots to see and do; the food is really
good (some dishes almost as hot as the weather!).
Today we visited the famous Golden Temple and
tomorrow we're going on an excursion to an island called
Ko Sichang.
Don't work too hard! See you when we get back.
                    Grill & Ruth
PS: Give our love to the big boss!

Dear Tanya,
Your father and I are spending a few days
here at the seaside. The weather has been
very wet so far, and unfortunately dad has
got a bad cold so we can't go out; not much
fresh air. We've seen some good programmes on
TV, though. Hope you're enjoying yourself in
London,
                    Mum

Dear Jo,
I'm sure you'll be surprised to get a card from me,
but here I am! Last night we spent our first night out
in the desert, and I must say it was fantastic. I
never knew there were so many stars. And that it
could be so quiet. I miss you, darling, and you know
I'll be back one day. I just need some time, that's
all. I hope you understand.
All my love,
                    K x

b Write a postcard from one of the places in part **a** to your teacher/someone in your class. Use some of the phrases from the box.

Hi, everyone !   See you when I/we get back
Dear ...   I'll be back soon / one day
We're spending a few days in ...
The weather has been ...
I can't believe we're here in ...   Don't work too hard
Here I am in ...   All my love   Lots to see ...
Hope you're enjoying yourself on ...   The food is ...
Give my/our love to ...   Today we visited ...
Tomorrow we're going to ...

Spelling
Words with *-ed* and *-ing*

LOOK!

Most of these words add *-ing* or *-ed* to the infinitive form.
interesting   *interested*

Words which end in *-e* **either**: drop the -e in the *-ing* form
come   *coming*
or: add *-d* in the *-ed* form
telephone   *telephoned*

Verbs which end in a consonant, a vowel and a consonant, double the final consonant in the *-ing* form.
put   *putting*

12 How do you spell the *-ing* and *-ed* form of these verbs?

a climb   *climbing*   *climbed*

b plan   _____   _____

c disgust   _____   _____

d surprise   _____   _____

e relax   _____   _____

f stay   _____   _____

g cycle   _____   _____

h move   _____   _____

Present perfect
Positive, negative and question forms

1 Complete the gaps in the dialogues below with a word from the box. Use each word **twice**.

've   's   have   has
haven't   hasn't

a   A: I' (1) _ve_____ just seen a

    friend of mine on TV.

    (2) _____ you ever

    appeared on television?

   B: No, but my brother

    (3) _____ . He was in a

    video a few years ago.

   A: Really? Was it good?

   B: I don't know. I

    (4) _____ seen it.

b   My friend Florence

   (5) _____ always wanted

   to be a successful writer. She

   (6) _____ written four

   novels, but she (7) _____

   made much money.

   I (8) _____ read any of

   them myself, but she tells me

   they're very exciting.

c   The Diamante Brothers

   (9) _____ been famous for

   more than twenty years. 'A show

   business life is the only life I

   (10) _____ known,' says

   Dion Diamante. 'It

   (11) _____ been easy for

   us to live a normal life. But it

   (12) _____ been a

   fantastic life ... so far!'

Present perfect and Past simple with *for*

2 Circle the best tense, Present perfect or Past simple.

a   The Earth *existed* / *has existed* for more than 4,000 million years.

b   Dinosaurs *have lived* / *lived* on Earth for 160 million years.

c   Humans *have been* / *were* on the planet for just 50,000 years.

d   In the past, people *thought* / *have thought* that the world was flat.

e   The first Australians – the Aborigines – *have lived* / *lived* there for about 40,000 years.

f   For many years, the USA *has been* / *was* a British colony.

g   The USA *has been* / *was* an independent country for over 200 years.

Present perfect: short answers

> **LOOK!**
>
> **Short answers with the Present perfect**
>
> Have I / you / we / they been to Japan?
>   Yes, I / you / we / they have.
>   No, I / you / we / they haven't.
>
> Has (s)he / it finished?
>   Yes, (s)he / it has.
>   No, (s)he / it hasn't.

3 Read the survey results and answer the questions. Use short answers.

	been to the USA?	passed driving test?	appeared on TV?
Rodolfo	✓	✓	✗
Hiroko	✗	✗	✗
Adam and Rachel	✓	✗	✓

a   Has Rodolfo been to the USA?   _Yes, he has._

b   Has Hiroko passed her driving test?   _No, she hasn't._

c   Has Rodolfo appeared on television?   _____

d   Has Hiroko been to the USA?   _____

e   Has Hiroko appeared on television?   _____

f   Have Adam and Rachel been to the USA?   _____

g   Have they passed their driving tests?   _____

h   Have they appeared on television?   _____

Present perfect with *just, yet, already* and *never*

> LOOK!
>
> We often use *just*, *never* and *already* with the Present perfect. These words come between *have* and the past participle.
>
> *They've **just** arrived.*
> *I've **already** done this exercise.*
> *I've **never** been to Australia.*
>
> *Yet* comes at the end of the sentence.
> *They haven't arrived **yet**.*

4 a Put *just*, *already*, *yet* or *never* in the right place in the 'B' sentences

1 A: What's the difference between Great Britain and the UK?
   B: I've/told you twice!
   already

2 A: Why are you looking so happy?
   B: I've heard that my cousin is coming to stay!

3 A: Do you like Thai food?
   B: I don't know. I've tried it.

4 A: Is Ernesto here?
   B: No, he hasn't arrived.

5 A: Would you like to go and see *X-Men* tonight?
   B: Not really, I've seen it twice.

b **T7.1** Listen and check. Practise saying the sentences.

Present perfect and Past simple with time phrases

5 In the sentences below, put the verb in brackets into the correct form: Present perfect or Past simple.

a Carlos _____*visited*_____ (visit) the USA about twelve years ago.

b _____ (go) to the cinema lately? No, I _____ (not/have) the time.

c The plane _____ (take off) at 8.15 … exactly on time.

d I _____ (never/see) anything so stupid in all my life!

e It _____ (be) a bad day in the shop: so far this morning we _____ (not/have) a single customer.

f My parents _____ (get married) when they _____ (be) only nineteen years old.

g I hope the weather gets better soon – it _____ (be) really terrible this week.

h Our son _____ (arrive) in Australia three weeks ago, but he _____ (write) to us yet.

i Caroline _____ (go) out a few minutes ago.

been or *gone*

> LOOK!
>
> *She's **gone** to school.* = She's at school, or on her way to school now.
>
> *She's **been** to school.* = She's not at school now.

6 Write *been* or *gone* in the following sentences.

a 'Where's Roberto?' 'He's _____*gone*_____ home.'

b I've _____ to South America three times in my life.

c 'I'm sorry, you can't speak to Erik – he's _____ out for lunch.'

d I left my umbrella here half an hour ago, and now it's _____ !

e How many times have you _____ to the supermarket this month?

f He's nearly forty years old, and he's never _____ abroad.

g Anna was here a minute ago. Where's she _____ ?

h Teresa is on her way to the station and Marc has _____ with her.

i Where have you _____ ? We've got to finish this work by 5.30.

43

Present perfect and Past simple

7 a Complete this text about Cher, using the correct tense, Present perfect or Past simple.

Few stars (1) __have had__ (have) careers as long and varied as Cher. In a career of more than three decades, she (2)_____ (be) successful both as a singer and as an actress.

Born Cherilyn Sarkasian LaPier in El Centro, California, on 20th May 1946, she (3)_____ (leave) home for Hollywood at the age of sixteen. When only seventeen she (4)_____ (marry) songwriter and record producer, Sonny Bono. As Sonny and Cher, they (5)_____ (have) several hits in the 1960s, including 'I Got You Babe' in 1964. But in the 1970s, success (6)_____ (be) more difficult to find, and Cher and Bono (7)_____ (get) divorced in 1975. Soon after, Cher (8)_____ (marry) rock star Gregg Allman, but the marriage only (9)_____ (last) until 1979. She (10)_____ (not / marry) again. Since the mid-1980s, Cher (11)_____ (have) a second career – as an actress, appearing in films like *The Witches of Eastwick* and *Faithful*. In 1988, she (12)_____ (win) a Best Actress Oscar for the film *Moonstruck*. More recently, Cher (13)_____ (return) to singing once more, and with great success – her single 'Believe' (14)_____ (become) US Number One in March 1999. In 2002, Cher (15)_____ (start) a farewell tour which (16)_____ (last) for over two years!

b **T7.2** Listen and check.

Past participles wordsearch

8 a There are twenty more irregular past participles in the box below. How many can you find? Write the past participle and the base form below.

1 _heard_   _hear_
2 _____ _____
3 _____ _____
4 _____ _____
5 _____ _____
6 _____ _____
7 _____ _____
8 _____ _____
9 _____ _____
10 _____ _____
11 _____ _____
12 _____ _____
13 _____ _____
14 _____ _____
15 _____ _____
16 _____ _____
17 _____ _____
18 _____ _____
19 _____ _____
20 _____ _____
21 _____ _____
22 _____ _____

H	E	A	R	D	R	B	S	A	T	C
M	A	D	E	O	C	R	E	K	S	O
W	T	O	L	D	S	O	E	T	P	M
R	E	S	O	L	D	U	N	C	O	E
I	N	E	S	U	N	G	F	O	K	D
T	P	U	T	N	C	H	O	S	E	N
T	D	R	U	N	K	T	U	T	N	T
E	G	O	T	G	W	O	N	Y	C	S
N	D	F	Y	P	A	I	D	D	A	W

b **T7.3** Listen and check. Practise saying the past participles.

Vocabulary
Ambitions and dreams

9 Complete the phrases with the correct verbs.

a _go_   ⎰ on a cruise
                 { to university
                 ⎱ abroad

b _____ ⎰ to speak a foreign language
                 { how to fly a plane
                 ⎱ how to drive a car

c _____ ⎰ a degree
                 { married
                 ⎱ a job

d _____ ⎰ a millionaire
                 { good at something
                 ⎱ famous

e _____ ⎰ an interesting job
                 { children
                 ⎱ a large family

f _____ ⎰ a musical instrument
                 { a sport
                 ⎱ in a band

g _____ ⎰ a novel
                 { a book
                 ⎱ a computer program

h _____ ⎰ a house or flat
                 { a car
                 ⎱ a holiday home

Pronunciation
The sounds /æ/ and /ʌ/

10 **a** **T7.4** We often pronounce the letter 'a' as /æ/. Listen to the example words. Underline the /æ/ sound.

married   family   language   Saturday

b **T7.5** We often pronounce the letter 'u' as /ʌ/. Listen to the example words. Underline the /ʌ/ sound.

country   just   understand   money

c **T7.6** Listen and write down the words you hear. Does each word have an /æ/ sound or an /ʌ/ sound?

1 _sat /æ/_
2 _____
3 _____
4 _____
5 _____
6 _____
7 _____
8 _____
9 _____
10 _____
11 _____
12 _____

d Listen again and practise saying the words.

Vocabulary booster: celebrity jobs

11 **a** Match the jobs in the pictures to the words in the box.

> fashion designer   film director   film star   international gymnast
> musician   pop star   professional footballer   supermodel
> TV chef   TV presenter

b 17.7 Listen and practise saying the words.

c Make **five** pairs of jobs which have something in common.

pop star and musician: both work in the music industry

Wordspot
for

12 Put *for* in the correct place in the sentences.

a Jan's been in Poland ∧ six
   months and she still doesn't
   speak any Polish!

b 'What are you looking?'
   'My wallet – I had it a moment
   ago.'

c Look – my husband gave me
   this lovely watch our wedding
   anniversary.

d Come on Sammy, it's ten
   o'clock, time bed.

e I read in a magazine yesterday
   that some diets are bad you.

f It's really hot today: do you
   want to go a swim?

g Excuse me, we ordered nearly
   an hour ago and we're still
   waiting our food.

h I opened this letter by mistake,
   it's you.

i Good morning! What would
   you like breakfast?

j Sitting in the sun for a long
   time isn't good your skin.

k I asked my boss a day off, but
   he said there's too much to do
   at the office.

l Hurry up! I don't want to be
   late the meeting.

Improve your writing
A mini-biography

13 a Read the text about jazz musician, Kenny G. Where should the phrases below go in the text?

A   As well as making records
B   He was born in 1956 as Kenny Gorelick in Seattle, USA
C   During the last twenty years, Kenny has played with
D   Kenny became well-known on the international music scene
E   When he was just fifteen years old
F   ~~Saxophonist Kenny G~~

Kenny G

The World's Favourite Jazz Musician ...

(1) _Saxophonist Kenny G_ . is now the world's most successful jazz musician.

(2) _____ , and he learned to play the saxophone at an early age. (3) _____ , he toured Europe with his high school band. After studying at Washington University he started his career as a musician. In 1982 he signed for Arista records and made his first solo album *Kenny G*.

Success came slowly at first, but during the 1990s (4) _____ . He released *Breathless*, his most successful album so far in 1993, and in 1994 won the Best Artist award at the 21st American Music Awards held in Los Angeles.

(5) _____ , he also found time to play in front of another famous saxophone player – US President Bill Clinton – at the 'Gala For The President' concert in Washington, and to break the world record for playing a single note (45 minutes and 47 seconds!) at the J & R Music World Store in New York in 1997.

(6) _____ superstars like Aretha Franklin, Michael Bolton and Whitney Houston and he has sold more than 36 million albums worldwide ... and he hasn't sung a note!

b Write some sentences about a famous musician, actor or entertainer from your country. Use these phrases to help you.

> ... is ... (*country's*) most successful ...
> He was born in ... (*place*) in ... (*year*)
> After ... he started his career as a ...
> He became well-known during ...
> When he was ... years old, he ...
> During the last ... years he has ... and ...

MODULE 8

Using articles
a or the

> **LOOK!**
> The first time we mention something, we use *a*.
> If we mention it again, we use *the*:
> *My uncle caught **a** big fish when he went fishing.*
> *Later, we cooked **the** fish for dinner.*

1 Complete the sentences with *a* or *the*.

a Jan's husband gave her _____ gold watch for her birthday.

b Julie and Sam have two children, _____ girl and _____ boy. _____ boy is seven and _____ girl is three.

c On Saturdays I work in _____ little shop in my village. _____ shop sells souvenirs, sweets and newspapers.

d China is _____ really interesting country. Have you been there?

e I bought _____ cheese sandwich and _____ cake for lunch. _____ cake was delicious but _____ sandwich tasted horrible.

Zero for general statements

2 **a** Find and cross out the unnecessary *the* in each sentence below.

a ~~The~~ Cola is one of the most popular drinks in the world.

b It's not true that English people drink the tea all the time.

c Drinking the coffee helps me to wake up in the morning!

d People in the Argentina often have a barbecue at the weekend.

e The Japanese tea isn't the same as English tea.

f Have you heard the news? The price of the petrol is going up again!

g Marco says that the best ice cream comes from the Italy.

h In the some parts of the United States, you can't drive until you're eighteen.

For general and specific statements

3 Look at the pairs of sentences and circle the correct phrase.

> **LOOK!**
> We do not use *the* when we talk about things or people **in general**.
> *Dogs make very good pets.*
>
> We use *the* to talk about **specific** things or people.
> *The people in my street are very friendly.*
> *'Where's the milk?' 'It's in the fridge.'*

a 'Where's *coffee* / (the coffee)?'
'It's in the cupboard on the left.'
I always drink (coffee) / *the coffee* at breakfast time.

b *Swiss people* / *The Swiss people* all learn two languages at school.
The Swiss people / *Swiss people* in my class all speak German.

c These days, it's easy to buy *books* / *the books* over the Internet.
Where are *books* / *the books* you borrowed from the library?

d What's *the weather* / *weather* like today?
Some people think that people work harder in *cold weather* / *the cold weather*.

e Can you pass me *salt* / *the salt* please?
Salt / *The salt* is bad for you if you eat too much of it.

f This river is so polluted that all *fish* / *the fish* have died.
Eating *fish* / *the fish* is very good for your heart.

g I went to see *Chicago* last night: *music* / *the music* was great!
I sometimes listen to *the music* / *music* when I'm working.

With geographical features

4 Read the Fact File about Japan. Complete the text using *the* or – .

(a) _____ – _____ Japan is not one island, but a group of over a thousand islands in (b) _____ Pacific Ocean, in the east of (c) _____ Asia. The four largest islands are (d) _____ Hokkaido, (e) _____ Honshu, (f) _____ Kyushu and (g) _____ Shikoku. Japan's nearest neighbours are (h) _____ North and South Korea across (i) _____ Sea of Japan, (j) _____ China and (k) _____ Russian Federation. There are a number of volcanic mountains, including (l) _____ Mount Fuji and (m) _____ Mount Aso. Other important mountain ranges are (n) _____ Chukogu Mountains and (o) _____ Japanese Alps not far from (p) _____ Nagoya, the third city. Hokkaido is the furthest north of the main islands. The main city is (q) _____ Sapporo on (r) _____ River Ishikari. Popular holiday places are (s) _____ Kitami Mountains and (t) _____ Lake Kussharo.

Japan: Fact file

Phrases with and without *the*

5 Complete the sentences with the correct preposition, with or without *the*.

a I don't want to go out tonight. I'd like to stay _____ home for a change.

b I never have anything to eat _____ morning, just a cup of coffee.

c There's a wonderful view of the city lights from this window _____ night.

d The most beautiful scenery is _____ north of the country.

e Marianne and her husband Tony first met when they were _____ school.

f If you take your car to England, don't forget to drive _____ left!

g There's a small village _____ bottom of the mountain.

h August is a very quiet time in the city – most people are _____ holiday.

i 'What did you study _____ university?' 'Economics and English.'

j I'd like to move out of the city and go and live _____ coast.

k Walk along Main Street for 200 metres, and you'll see the railway station _____ right.

l 'Can I speak to Joel please?' 'I'm afraid he's still _____ bed!'

m Here's my office telephone number if you want to ring me _____ work.

n Of all the hotels _____ centre of the city, I think the Metropole is the best.

Quantifiers with countable and uncountable nouns *some*, *any* and *no*

6 Complete the sentences with *some*, *any* or *no*.

a   Helga can't work abroad because she doesn't speak ____*any*____ foreign languages.

b   Would you like _____ more coffee before you leave?

c   There are _____ letters for you over there, on the table.

d   Do you have _____ questions you'd like to ask me?

e   If there are _____ more questions, we can finish now.

f   I'm afraid there's _____ ice cream in the fridge. How about _____ fruit instead?

g   Can you buy _____ bread when you go to the supermarket?

h   I can't get a ticket from the machine – I haven't got _____ change.

i   There are _____ food shops open in the village on a Sunday, so you'll have to eat in a restaurant.

much, many, a lot of, a few, no

7 a   Look at the picture of Luke's bedroom. Complete the sentences about Luke using the words in the box.

much	many	a lot of	a few	no	a

1   There isn't _____*much*_____ space in his bedroom.

2   He hasn't got _____ books.

3   He's got _____ work to do!

4   He's got _____ videos.

5   There are _____ pictures on the wall.

6   There is _____ water in the bottle.

7   He's got _____ computer, and _____ computer games.

8   There are _____ plants in his room.

b   **T8.1**   Listen and check. Practise saying the sentences.

much, many, too much, too many and *not enough*

8 Complete the sentences using *much*, *many*, *too much*, *too many* or *enough*. Which sentences are true for you?

a I don't have very ___much___ free time during the week.

b I know that I eat _____ chocolate and _____ cakes.

c I don't usually do _____ exercise – unless I have to run for the bus!

d I feel really tired because I didn't have _____ sleep last night.

e I don't know _____ people who speak English well.

f I don't have _____ money to go on holiday this year so I'll have to stay at home.

g I've got _____ things to do today: I won't be able to do them all.

h I don't like coffee which has _____ sugar in it.

i I don't think I've made _____ mistakes in this exercise!

Vocabulary
Geographical features

9 Choose a word from the box to complete the sentences.

the coastline canals volcanoes lakes deserts borders mountain ranges islands the climate ~~rivers~~

a Bridges go over them; fish live in them; they always go to the sea. __rivers__

b Camels like them; they are very dry and often hot; you don't need an umbrella in them. _____

c It can be hot or cold, wet or dry, you can't change it! _____

d You can swim in them and sail or windsurf on them. _____

e They can be big or small; Ireland is one; they have water all around them. _____

f They can be dangerous; sometimes they get very hot; Sicily has a famous one. _____

g You have to cross them to get from one country to another. _____

h It's next to the sea; it can be rocky; you can see it from the air. _____

i They're usually straight; boats sail on them; Venice is famous for them. _____

j They cover a lot of space; they can divide countries; sometimes you can drive over them. _____

Vocabulary booster: things you find in cities

10 **a** Write the words for the pictures.

a bridge   a fountain   skyscrapers   ~~a statue~~
a mosque   a motorway   a market   a square
a church   a bus station   a park   an art gallery

1 __a statue__	7 _____
2 _____	8 _____
3 _____	9 _____
4 _____	10 _____
5 _____	11 _____
6 _____	12 _____

b **T8.2** Listen and check. Practise saying the words.

c Divide the words into **four** categories.

Buildings	Transport	Open spaces	Other
a church	_____	_____	_____
_____	_____	_____	_____
_____	_____	_____	_____
_____	_____	_____	_____

Listen and read

11 a **T8.3** Read and listen to the text about volcanoes.

Volcanoes

escaping gases
lava
rock

We have all seen pictures like this from time to time ...
perhaps you live in a country where there are volcanoes.

Here are some of the most frequently asked questions about volcanoes.

What are volcanoes?

A volcano is a mountain or hill with an opening through which steam, gases and lava from the centre of the Earth can escape into the air.

What is lava?

Lava is red-hot rock which comes to the Earth's surface through the volcano. It has a temperature of about 1,000°C – ten times hotter than boiling water! Lava can move as fast as 55 kph ... faster than most animals can run.

How many volcanoes are there in the world?

There are about 850 active volcanoes in the world. About sixty percent are in an area called the Ring of Fire in the Pacific Ocean. The largest active volcano is Mauna Loa on the island of Hawaii.

What's the difference between 'active' and 'extinct' volcanoes?

An active volcano can erupt at any time. Extinct volcanoes are volcanoes that have stopped erupting.

What happens when they erupt?

A volcano erupts when there is a violent escape of gases and lava from the volcano. In 79 AD, Mount Vesuvius in Italy erupted, destroying the Roman city of Pompeii. The worst volcanic disaster in the twentieth century was in Martinique, a French island in the Caribbean Sea. A volcano called Mount Pelée near the town of St Pierre erupted on the morning of 8th May 1902. Of the 30,000 people in St Pierre, just two survived.

Can we predict when a volcano is going to erupt?

Nowadays, scientists usually know when a volcano is going to erupt. In 1991, the Pinatubo volcano,100 kilometres northwest of Manila in the Philippines, began one of the largest eruptions of the twentieth century. Thanks to the scientists' warnings, more than 100,000 people left the area before the volcano erupted on 15th June.

b **Complete the notes below with a name or number.**

1 temperature of lava
   1,000°C
   _____

2 speed at which lava can move
   _____

3 number of active volcanoes in the world
   _____

4 percentage of volcanoes which are in the Ring of Fire
   _____

5 location of Mauna Loa
   _____

6 date when Mount Vesuvius erupted
   _____

7 location of Martinique
   _____

8 date when Mount Pelée erupted
   _____

9 number of people in St Pierre who died
   _____

10 number of people who survived
   _____

11 year when Pinatubo erupted
   _____

12 number of people who escaped
   _____

Pronunciation
Compounds with two nouns

> **LOOK!**
>
> In English, there are many nouns made of two words (compound nouns). Notice the stress on the first word:
>
> | noun + noun: | petrol + station | ⇨ | petrol station |
> | -ing form + noun: | dining + room | ⇨ | dining room |

12 **T8.4** Mark the stress on these compound nouns. Then listen and check.

a   bus stop
b   motorway
c   telephone number
d   railway station
e   skyscraper
f   bedroom
g   computer game
h   art gallery

Real life
Asking for and giving directions

13 a Correct the mistake in each of the sentences below.

1   Excuse me, I'm looking Praed Street.
2   Can you give me some direction?
3   There's a post office on the corner. You can miss it.
4   How I can get to the hospital, please?
5   Carry past the supermarket and it's on your right.
6   How long time does it take to walk?
7   Walk Randall Street until you get to the library.
8   Turn right at end of this street, and I think that's Park Road.

b   Put **five** of the sentences in part a in the correct place in the conversations.

1   A: _____
    B: About twenty minutes, I'd say.

2   A: _____
    B: I can try. Where do you want to go?

3   A: Excuse me, do you know where Park Road is?
    B: _____

4   A: Excuse me, where's the nearest post office?
    B: Go down to the end of this street: _____

5   A: _____
    B: Turn left just after the cafe – look, where that ambulance is going.

Improve your writing
Notes giving directions

14 Look at the directions on pages 77 and 78 of the Students' Book. Write full sentences for the notes below.

a   get off train / St Christopher's Station
    Get off the train at St Christopher's Station.

b   come out of station / turn left
    _____

c   walk / Station Road / about fifty metres
    _____

d   there / bus stop / on / right. Take / number 11 bus / to Sandy Bay
    _____

e   get off / see large petrol station / on corner
    _____

f   cross road / walk about 100 metres
    _____

g   take / first turning / left, where / see sign saying 'Holiday Apartments'
    _____

h   down hill towards sea / see 'Holiday Apartments' office on right. / open 9–5
    _____

Spelling
Same pronunciation, different spelling (homophones)

15 a Many words in English have the same pronunciation, but different spelling and meaning:
There were **two** people sitting in the square.
It was **too** dark to see anything.

b   Underline the correct spelling of each word in the text below.

> If you need to buy something to eat, there's a [1]*knew/new* restaurant quite near [2]*hear/here* which you could try: we [3]*ate/eight* there last week and had a very good meal. When you come out of the house, turn [4]*right/write*. Walk along the [5]*road/rode* for about a 100 metres, [6]*passed/past* the bank, and you'll [7]*sea/see* the restaurant on the corner. Make sure you get [8]*their/there* early, because the restaurant always gets very full [9]*buy/by* about [10]*ate/eight* o'clock.

may, might, will, definitely, etc.
will/won't

1 **a** On 31st December 1999, Madame Sol – a world famous astrologer – made some predictions for the next ten years. Write out the sentences using *will/won't*.

1 There / be / a woman president of the United States

   There will be a woman president of the

   United States.

2 People / not use / cash / they / only use / credit cards

   _____

   _____

   _____

3 Astronauts / visit / the planet Mars

   _____

   _____

   _____

4 Great Britain / not have / a king or queen

   _____

   _____

   _____

5 The countries of Western Europe / all use / the same currency

   _____

   _____

   _____

6 A terrible bug / destroy / the world's computers

   _____

   _____

   _____

b Write some predictions of your own about the next ten years, using the ideas in the sentences in part **a**.

There won't be a woman president in my country

in the next ten years.

will probably / probably won't

2 Doctors believe that about 355,500 babies were born all around the world on New Year's Day 2000. New Zealand had the first Millennium baby. What can we predict about his life in the third millennium? Complete each sentence with *will definitely/probably* or *definitely/probably won't*.

a He _will probably_ have a completely normal life.

b He _____ remember the Millennium celebrations.

c He _____ be famous all his life.

d He _____ be alive in the year 3000.

e He _____ see a lot of changes in the third millennium.

f He _____ speak English when he's older.

g His parents _____ become rich.

h People around the world _____ forget about him in a few years.

may/might

3 Rewrite the sentences using *may (not)* or *might (not)* instead of the phrase in bold.

a **It's possible that** Martin **will** be at Sally's party on Saturday.

Martin may/might be at
Sally's party on Saturday.

b **Maybe** we **will** go abroad for our holidays next year.

_____
_____

c **Perhaps** they **won't** be able to finish the work until next week.

_____
_____

d Take your coat; **it's possible that** it **will** get cold later.

_____
_____

e **Maybe** your mother **won't** want to go out this evening.

_____
_____

f **Perhaps** Martha **will not** be able to help you.

_____
_____

g **Maybe** the Prime Minister **will** resign if things don't get better.

_____
_____

h Buy a lottery ticket: **it's possible that** you'll win £1 million!

_____
_____

will/won't/may/might

4 a Read the daily horoscope opposite. Which sign:

1 may have family problems?
Cancer

2 will have a good day at school?
_____

3 might need more money than usual? _____

4 will have more things to do than usual? _____

5 may get very angry?
_____

O <u>*Yesterday*</u>

O <u>*Send this horoscope*</u>
<u>*to a friend*</u>

O <u>*Tomorrow*</u>

Your Daily Horoscope for Wednesday 17 May
by *__Sylvia Fox__*

Taurus

You might have an argument with an important person today. If this happens, you'll need help. A friend or partner will be very useful to you. And who knows ... you might win the argument!

Gemini

This will be another busy work day for you: you'll have all the normal things to do, but there may also be an extra job or two. But don't worry, you'll succeed! And think how happy you'll be when you finish!

Cancer

You may have to choose between your public and your private life today. You won't spend much time with your loved ones until later in the week. Make sure they know you love them, or they may feel forgotten.

Leo

This will be your lucky day for education! If you're still at school, it'll be a good day for study – something you've always thought was too hard for you will be easy. If you've already left school, think about going back to your studies – you won't regret it!

Virgo

There will be some money worries today. Check what you're spending – you may need to spend some extra money on travel, but if you buy something for a loved one, they may not thank you for it!

b Underline all the examples of predictions in the text.

c **T9.1** Listen to some of the predictions. Practise saying the sentences.

55

Present tense after *if*, *when*, *before* and other time words
Present tense after *if*

5 Match the beginnings of the sentences in A with the endings in B and write out the complete sentences.

A

a   If the weather / be / good this weekend
b   If you / work / hard
c   If you / be / late for class again
d   If you / not get up / soon
e   If the train / arrive / on time
f   If you / not take / a map
g   If we / see / a restaurant

B

you / pass / all your exams
we / be / home before midnight
you / get / lost
your teacher / get / very annoyed
we / have / a barbecue
we / stop / for lunch
you / be / late for class

a   *If the weather's good this weekend, we'll have a barbecue.*

b   _____

c   _____

d   _____

e   _____

f   _____

g   _____

Time clauses: *if, when, before, as soon as*

6 Circle the best way to complete each sentence.

a   I promise to telephone you *as soon as* / *before* / *if* I arrive.

b   *As soon as* / *If* / *When* you don't leave me alone, I'll call the police!

c   What are you going to do *as soon as* / *if* / *when* you finish university?

d   If we drive quickly, we'll probably get home *before* / *if* / *when* it gets dark.

e   This exam is very important for Margaret; *as soon as* / *if* / *when* she passes, she can go to university.

f   'Please check you have all your luggage *as soon as* / *if* / *when* you leave the train.'

g   *As soon as* / *Before* / *If* you go, could you give me your e-mail address?

h   Promise to tell me the news *as soon as* / *before* / *if* you hear anything.

i   I'm sure I'll be married *as soon as* / *if* / *when* I'm thirty.

Word order

7 Put the words in the correct order to make sentences.

a will / win / probably / I / Germany / think / the football match.
  I think Germany will probably win the football match.

b be / There / won't / any / tonight / snow / definitely

  _____

c will / tomorrow / be / Stefan / definitely / at home

  _____

d the answer / know / probably / to your question / won't / He

  _____

e able / will / We / next week / be / to give / definitely / you / an answer

  _____

Vocabulary
Modern and traditional

8 **a** Put the words in the box into one of the categories below.

cash   a stove   a credit card   a text message   book online central heating   a letter   play computer games   a microwave oven download files   a coal fire   queue up for tickets   an electric fan a charge card   a street market   a dishwasher   a fax   air conditioning a shopping mall   a washing machine

1 places where you go shopping: _____ _____

2 things you can do on a computer: _____ _____

  _____

3 things in the kitchen: _____ _____

  _____ _____

4 things you can send: _____ _____

  _____

5 things you can pay with: _____ _____

  _____

6 things that keep you warm: _____ _____

7 things that keep you cool: _____ _____

8 something you might do outside the cinema: _____

b Complete the sentences with a word or phrase from the box.

1 It's quicker to cook food in a _____ than in a normal oven.

2 It's fun to go shopping in a _____ if the weather's good.

3 Can you turn that _____ off, please? It's blowing all my papers off my desk.

4 There are some clean glasses in the _____ : it's just finished.

5 That store offered me a _____ , but their interest rates are really high.

Pronunciation
The letter 'i'

9 **a** The letter 'i' can be pronounced:

/ɪ/ as in *big*   /aɪ/ as in *microwave*

b **T9.2** How do we pronounce the 'i' in these words? Listen and check. Write /ɪ/ or /aɪ/ for each word.

1 file _/aɪ/_

2 traditional _____

3 nightmare _____

4 credit _____

5 definitely _____

6 mind _____

7 online _____

8 decision _____

9 mobile _____

10 equipment _____

11 might _____

12 electric _____

c Listen again and practise saying the words.

Vocabulary booster: technology

10 **a** Label the items in the shop window with a word from the box.

answering machine   keyboard   laptop   computer   mouse mat   screen
mouse   digital camera   video recorder   printer

b **T9.3** Listen to the pronunciation of the words. Practise saying them.

c Which of the items:

1   needs paper? _____

2   can you record something on? _____ _____

3   do you connect to a computer? _____ _____ _____ _____ _____

4   do you carry around with you? _____ _____

5   is the smallest? _____

Wordspot
if

 11 Complete the sentences with *if* and a word or phrase from the box.

I asked my teacher	Do you mind
Does anyone know	possible
I wonder	you like
I don't know	I were you
necessary	What

a _____ I open this window? It's so hot in here.

b We'd like to have a room with a balcony and a sea view, _____ .

c _____ the number 455 bus has gone yet?

d I'll cook dinner tonight, _____ .

e _____ , I'd have some lessons before you take your driving test.

f _____ I had passed the exam, but she didn't answer!

g _____ my husband has remembered that it's Valentine's Day tomorrow.

h 'What about the Carlyle report?' 'Well, _____ I can work late this evening and finish it.'

i _____ it rains on the day of the picnic?

j _____ I'll be able to mend your bike, but I'll try.

Improve your writing
Saying thank you

 12 a Look at the letter and e-mail.

- Which one is to thank someone for a birthday present?
- Which one is from the owner of the Paradiso Café?

A

> Paradiso Café
> Elm Street
>
> 2.4.05
>
> Dear Maria, Gerard, Kurt and Minako,
> I am writing to thank you for the wonderful job you did on the café. It is like a completely different place. Since its 'facelift', the number of customers has kept going up and up, and we now have regular customers who comment on the warm and welcoming atmosphere, the comfortable armchairs and the soft lighting and music. I hope you will all be able to come and have lunch here one day next week: <u>on the house</u>, of course. The menu you designed is very popular – especially the chocolate cake and the home-made ice cream!
>
> Thank you once again,
>
> George Prados

Glossary *on the house* means you don't have to pay

B
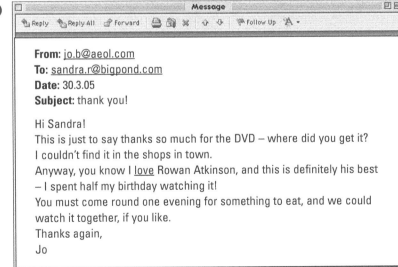

From: jo.b@aeol.com
To: sandra.r@bigpond.com
Date: 30.3.05
Subject: thank you!

Hi Sandra!
This is just to say thanks so much for the DVD – where did you get it? I couldn't find it in the shops in town.
Anyway, you know I <u>love</u> Rowan Atkinson, and this is definitely his best – I spent half my birthday watching it!
You must come round one evening for something to eat, and we could watch it together, if you like.
Thanks again,
Jo

b Put these parts of the thank you letters in order:

saying why they are pleased with the present or with what the other person did ☐

saying thank you again ☐

saying why they are writing ☐

inviting the other person to do something ☐

c Write a letter to someone for a present you received or for something he/she did for you.

used to

used to / didn't use to

1 Roger Curry lives with his wife and three children in a castle in Scotland. He drives a Rolls Royce car, has a private plane and always wears expensive designer clothes. But things weren't always so good for Roger. Write six sentences with *used to* and one of the verbs in the box.

wear	have	be	work

a   *He used to have long hair.* _____ (long hair)
b   _____ (moustache)
c   _____ (old T-shirt)
d   _____ (a very boring job)
e   _____ (hamburger restaurant)
f   _____ (poor)

2 Write some negative sentences about Roger Curry using the words in brackets.

a   (be / rich)
    He didn't use to be rich. _____

b   (live / Scotland)
    _____

c   (drive / Rolls Royce)
    _____

d   (have / private plane)
    _____

e   (wear / designer clothes)
    _____

f   (have / good life)
    _____

3 Rewrite the sentences with *used to* where possible.

a   As a child I was very healthy. I didn't have many colds, and I only went to hospital once, when I broke my leg.
    As a child I was very healthy. I didn't use to have
    many colds and I only went to hospital once,
    when I broke my leg.

b   Claudia had a bicycle, but she sold it when her parents gave her a motorbike.
    _____
    _____

c   My little brother hated vegetables. He always put them on my plate when I wasn't looking!
    _____
    _____

d   Last weekend we stayed in a little hotel by the sea, where I stayed every year on family holidays.
    _____
    _____

e   There was a sweet shop on the corner of the street: I remember we bought sweets on the way home from school every day.
    _____
    _____

f   There weren't many fast food restaurants in this town twenty years ago – now there are at least ten!
    _____
    _____

Past continuous

Important moments in history

4 Complete these sentences using the Past continuous form of the verbs in brackets.

When SS *Titanic* hit the iceberg ...

a   people _*were dancing*_ (dance) in the ballroom.
b   the captain _____ (read) a book in his cabin.

When John Lennon met Paul McCartney ...

c   John _____ (play) with a group called *The Quarrymen*.
d   rock 'n' roll music _____ (become) popular in England.

When Neil Armstrong first walked on the moon ...

e the other astronauts _____ (sit) inside Apollo eleven.

f millions of people _____ (watch) it on television.

When Nelson Mandela left prison ...

g his wife Winnie _____ (wait) for him.

h his supporters _____ (sing) outside the prison.

Past continuous and Past simple

5 a Put the verb in the correct tense, Past continuous or Past simple.

1 I _____ (watch) TV at home, when someone _____ (come) to the door.

2 My mother _____ (phone) while I _____ (prepare) dinner.

3 When we _____ (arrive) home, some friends _____ (wait) for us.

4 As I _____ (walk) along the street, I _____ (see) an old friend.

5 When I _____ (wake) up, everyone _____ (look) at me.

6 Jane _____ (see) another guest who _____ (wear) exactly the same hat!

b **T10.1** Listen and check. Practise saying the sentences.

6 Read the story of when Dave Mascott met his hero, and put the verb in brackets in the Past simple or Past continuous.

The famous American rock star Bob Goldhart
(a) ___was doing___ (do) a tour of Britain when he
(b) _____ (meet) British rock star Dave
Wells at a party. As he (c) _____ (leave),
Dave (d) _____ (invite) Bob to come to his
house and (e) _____ (tell) him the address.
But Bob (f) _____ (made) a
mistake as he (g) _____ (write) down the
address: he wrote 'Addison Street' instead of 'Addison
Road'.

The next day, Helen Mascott of 145 Addison Street,
London (h) _____ (listen) to the radio in her
kitchen when the doorbell (i) _____ (ring). A
man with long hair (j) _____ (stand) outside.
She (k) _____ (think) the man
(l) _____ (look) familiar but
(m) _____ (not say) anything.
'Is Dave in?' the man (n) _____ (ask)
politely. The woman – whose husband's name was also
Dave – (o) _____ (explain) that Dave
(p) _____ (do) the shopping, but he would
be back in a few minutes.

She (q) _____ (invite) Bob Goldhart to come
in and wait. While Helen (r) _____ (make)
some coffee, he (s) _____ (look) around the
living room and (t) _____ (be) very happy to
see all of his albums!

A few minutes later, Dave (u) _____ (arrive)
home. 'You've got a visitor,' Helen
(v) _____ (tell) her husband.
When Dave – a big, big fan of Bob Goldhart –
(w) _____ (open) the living room door and
(x) _____ (see) who
(y) _____ (wait) for him ... he
(z) _____ (faint)!

Questions and short answers

> **Questions and short answers with the Past continuous**
>
> Was I / (s)he / it going?
>   Yes, I / (s)he / it was.
>   No, I / (s)he / it wasn't.
>
> Were you / we / they going?
>   Yes, you / we / they were.
>   No, you / we / they weren't.

7 Complete the conversation with the correct form of the verb in brackets, or with a short answer.

PO = Police Officer   MR A = Mr Adams

PO: Now, Mr Adams, what (a) __were you doing__ (you / do) between 7 and 9 p.m. last night?

MR A: (b) _____ (I / watch) a film at the Odeon Cinema.

PO: (c) _____ (your wife and children / watch) it with you?

MR A: No, (d) _____ .

PO: What (e) _____ (they / do)?

MR A: (f) _____ (they / visit) my mother-in-law.

PO: I see. Now, (g) _____ (it / rain) when you went into the cinema?

MR A: Yes, (h)_____ .

PO: (i) _____ (you / carry) an umbrella?

MR A: No, (j)_____ .

PO: Hmm. What about when you left the cinema, (k) _____ (it / rain) then?

MR A: Yes, I mean, no, (l) _____ .

PO: And (m) _____ (your wife / wait) for you outside?

MR A: No, of course (n) _____ .

PO: I think you're lying. Someone saw you outside the cinema, in the rain, carrying an umbrella, with your wife – and it was 7.30 p.m!

Vocabulary
Health and accidents

8 Complete the sentences with a word from the box.

> allergic   antibiotics   bandage   ~~burn~~
> come round   dizzy   faints   plaster   rash
> sting   swelling   symptoms

a   Be careful not to ___burn___ yourself when you use the iron.

b   Has anyone got a _____ ? I've cut my finger.

c   My mum always _____ when she sees a spider. Last time I had to throw a bucket of water at her to make her _____ .

d   The doctor gave me some _____ but I forgot to take them yesterday.

e   Let's take the _____ off your ankle: hm, there's still a lot of _____ from the fall.

f   I think I'm _____ to the washing powder. I've got this horrible _____ all over my back.

g   Where exactly did the bee _____ you? I can't see anything.

h   A: Describe your _____ to me, Mr Arnold.
    B: Well, I feel _____ all the time – as if the room's moving round me.

Verb + noun/adjective combinations

9 Complete the phrases with the correct verbs.

a   _____ { an aspirin / pills / a course of antibiotics

b   _____ { a plaster / some cream   on it. / a bandage

c   _____ { warm / cool / calm

d   _____ { a rash / a temperature / a cold

e   _____ { sick / dizzy / better

Vocabulary booster: at the doctor's

10

a Which person in the picture:

has got a bad cold?	10	has got a bruise?	
has cut himself?		has got a stomach ache?	
has got a toothache?		has broken his leg?	
is bleeding?		has got backache?	
has got a bad headache?		is coughing?	
is sneezing?		has got a swollen hand?	

b Label the picture.

Waiting Room

1 ____

2 ____

3 ____

4 ____

5 ____

6 ____

7 ____

8 ____

9 ____

10
He has a bad cold
____

c T10.2 Listen and check. Practise saying the phrases.

Flying Doctors

When baby Thomas James Ellis grows up, he will have a great story to tell his grandchildren about the day he was born.

On Tuesday 6 January 2004, Thomas was born several weeks early on a Flying Doctor aircraft as it landed at Tamworth Airport. Thomas' parents, Genienne and James Ellis, live in the <u>outback</u>, a long way from any towns.

'This is the third time the Flying Doctors have come to my aid. It's a wonderful organisation and I don't know what I would have done without them,' Genienne said.

The Flying Doctor service started in 1928. It was the idea of Reverend John Flynn, a church minister who was working in the Australian outback. He had many stories to tell about how necessary an aerial medical service was, including one about Jimmy Darcy. Jimmy had a bad fall, and it took his friends twelve hours to take him thirty miles to the nearest town. The only person there who knew first aid was the Postmaster, and he performed a seven-hour operation without anaesthetic, following instructions in <u>Morse code</u> from his first aid teacher, who was 2,000 miles away. Unfortunately, Jimmy died ten days later.

In May 1928, Dr St Vincent Welch made the first official flying doctor visit. In the following year he saw 255 patients. He had no radio, and used a compass and landmarks like rivers and fences to find his way. Nowadays the Royal Flying Doctor Service has forty-six planes, attends about 500 patients each day and services an area of 7,150,000 square kilometres. The service is available twenty-four hours a day, 365 days a year. Modern technology is also available: the doctors have digital cameras and video conferencing facilities. However, a pilot might still need the help of ordinary people on the ground when he is landing the plane in the outback: sometimes he asks them to do a 'roo run', which means driving up and down the landing area to frighten off kangaroos and other wild animals!

People who have never been to Australia have often heard of the Flying Doctors. In the 1980s a TV series was made about them, and shown in fifty countries. Also, next time you have an Australian $20 note, look more closely – the Flying Doctors and their founder, John Flynn, are on one 'face' of the note.

Glossary

outback is countryside far from towns, where few people live

Morse code is a way of sending messages using dots (...) and dashes (- -)

Listen and read

11 T10.3 Read and/or listen to the text opposite about the Flying Doctors of Australia. What do the numbers in the box refer to? Match a number to a fact from the text.

1928	20	7
500	24	2004
3	50	255
12		

a   The number of hours per day that the Flying Doctor service is available.

_____

b   The number of times that the Flying Doctors have helped Genienne Ellis.

_____

c   The year that the Flying Doctors started.

_____

d   The number of countries that had the Flying Doctors TV series.

_____

e   The number of patients visited in the first year of the service.

_____

f   The number of hours that the operation on Jimmy Darcy lasted.

_____

g   The year that Thomas Ellis was born.

_____

h   The value in dollars of the note with the picture of the Flying Doctors on it.

_____

i   The number of hours that it took Jimmy Darcy's friends to travel thirty miles.

_____

j   The number of patients that the Flying Doctors see every day.

_____

Pronunciation
The letter 'c'

12 a   How do we pronounce 'c' and 'ch' in these words?

LOOK!

Before *e* and *i* we usually pronounce *c* as /s/: *circle*

Before *a*, *o* and *u* we usually pronounce *c* as /k/: *cough*

We usually pronounce *ch* as /tʃ/: *chair*

In some words we pronounce *ch* as /k/: *stomach*

1	medicine	/s/	7	backache	_____
2	headache	_____	8	children	_____
3	electricity	_____	9	school	_____
4	exercise	_____	10	chest	_____
5	century	_____	11	cure	_____
6	crash	_____	12	accident	_____

b   T10.4 Listen and check. Practise saying the words.

Improve your writing
Time phrases

13 Complete the sentences with a time phrase from the box.

always	as	as quickly as possible	at the age of seventy	eventually
immediately	~~later~~	soon	then	until	

a   Jeff and Carla argued and Carla ended their engagement. ___Later___ , Carla was sorry and asked Jeff to come back.

b   I won't leave _____ you tell me exactly what happened.

c   My mother _____ told me that I would be rich and famous one day, but I didn't believe her.

d   We waited nearly twenty minutes by the side of the road. _____ a car stopped.

e   My grandfather is amazing: _____ he still goes for a swim every morning.

f   This is for you. I noticed it _____ I was passing the jeweller's. Do you like it?

g   Please come _____ . There's been an accident!

h   Joe was so tired that when he got home he went to bed _____ .

i   It started snowing heavily in the afternoon and _____ everything was covered in white.

j   Gwen put her necklace back in its box. _____ she noticed that her diamond ring was missing.

Gerunds (-ing forms) after verbs of liking and disliking

1 Use the prompts in box A and the sentence endings in box B to write sentences that are true for you.

A

look / after young children   walk / in the country
drive / very fast   sunbathe   work / on a computer
swim / in the sea   jog   go / to the gym
travel / by plane   study / English   climb / mountains
drive / on the motorway

B

... helps you to relax   ... is very boring
... makes you tired   ... is good for you
... is hard work   ... is good fun   ... is dangerous
... is bad for you

Looking after young children is good fun.

Looking after young children is hard work.

Gerunds after prepositions

2 **a** Rewrite the sentences, using the words in brackets. Keep the meaning the same.

1 Jack really loves surfing the Internet. (crazy about)

   Jack is crazy about surfing the Internet.

2 When I was young, collecting stamps interested me. (interested in)

3 I'm very sorry, I just can't remember people's names! (not good at)

4 They left the restaurant; they didn't pay the bill. (without)

5 Why don't you do something and not just sit there? (instead of)

6 Does walking alone at night frighten you? (frightened of)

7 Katrina doesn't think about anything except making money. (obsessed with)

8 My father didn't have a problem with lending me the car. (OK about)

9 My sister loves shopping for clothes. (mad about)

10 My husband doesn't like shopping for clothes very much. (not very keen on)

b **T11.1** Listen and check. Practise saying the sentences.

Verbs of liking and disliking

3 The symbols on the table show what two children think of the things below. Write sentences to describe how they feel, using the phrases in the box.

really loves	doesn't mind	it's OK
doesn't really like	really hates	is keen on
is not very keen on	really enjoys/likes	
is crazy about	can't stand	likes

		Joseph	Jessica
a	maths	☺ ☺	☹ ☹
b	playing football	☺	☺
c	singing	☹ ☹	☺
d	reading	☺ ☺	☺ ☺
e	playing computer games	☺ ☺	☹
f	cooking	😐	☺ ☺
g	chocolate	☺	☺
h	doing homework	☹	😐

a <u>Joseph really likes maths, but Jessica can't stand it.</u>

b <u>They both like playing football. / They are both</u>
<u>keen on playing football.</u>

c _____
_____

d _____
_____

e _____
_____

f _____
_____

g _____
_____

h _____
_____

like doing and *would like to do*

4 **a** Circle the best form: *like* or *would like* to complete the sentences below.

1 What do you think Ian (would like) / likes for his birthday?

2 Annette *likes / would like* Brad Pitt so much, she's got all his films on video.

3 *I'd like to speak / I like speaking* to Mr Shizuko, please.

4 *Would you like to go / Do you like going* for a coffee after class today?

5 One day, I *love going / would love to go* to Florida.

6 Jenny always drives to college because *she doesn't like walking / she wouldn't like to walk.*

7 I *would love to be / love being* a professional ballet dancer, but I'm too tall.

8 It's late and *I'd like to go / I like going* home. Can you phone for a taxi?

b **T11.2** Listen and check.

5 Read about Christopher Coleman. Correct the verbs in bold which should be in the *-ing* form.

Being
(a)**Be** addicted to something isn't so unusual; some people can't (b)**live** without (c)**smoke**; others enjoy (d)**shop**; many people say they are addicted to (e)**eat** chocolate; but Christopher Coleman has a more unusual addiction.

'I've always loved (f)**drink** cola,' he said, 'but a few years ago I began (g)**buy** more and more. I couldn't (h)**sleep** at night, and I needed five cans in the morning to stop (i)**shake**! In a normal day, I drank about forty cans. (j)**Get** enough cola every day was the only important thing in life! My girlfriend told me to stop (k)**spend** all my money on cola, but I didn't (l)**listen**. So in the end, she left me.

Would you like ...? and *Do you like ...?*: short answers

> Would you like to travel round the world?
>   Yes, I would.
>   No, I wouldn't.
>
> Would you like to come to my party?
>   Yes, I'd love to.
>   I'm afraid   I can't.
>   I'm busy.
>
> Do you like   swimming?
>   chocolate?
>   Yes, I do. / Yes, I love it.
>   No, I don't. / No, I hate it.
>   It's OK.
>
> Do you like cats?
>   Yes, I do. / Yes, I love them.
>   No, I don't. / No, I hate them.
>   They're OK.

LOOK!

6 a Choose an answer from the box below for each question.

> No, I hate it. It all sounds the same.
> Yes, I'd love to. What's on?
> It's OK. I'm not very good at it.
> No, I wouldn't. Two children are enough!
> I don't know, I've never tried them!
> That's a nice idea, but I'm afraid I've brought sandwiches.

1 Would you like to go out for lunch?
   _____

2 Do you like windsurfing?
   _____

3 Would you like to have a big family?
   _____

4 Do you like toffee apples?
   _____

5 Do you like rap music?
   _____

6 Would you like to go to see the film with me?
   _____

b Answer these questions about yourself.

1 Would you like to fly a helicopter?
2 Do you like dancing?
3 Would you like to appear on TV?
4 Do you like rain?

Vocabulary
Hobbies and interests

7 Read the clues and complete the words.

a They are both board games; two people can play.
   c _ _ _ _ and b _ _ _ _ _ _ _ _

b You try to watch them every week, whether they are playing at home or away.
   your f _ _ _ _ _ _ _ _ f _ _ _ _ _ _ _ t _ _ _

c You collect them, but you don't use them to buy things.
   c _ _ _ _

d You can take them off your old letters or you can buy special ones at the Post Office.
   s _ _ _ _ _

e You can make them out of plastic, wood, or even paper. People often make boats or aeroplanes.
   m _ _ _ _ _

f You can comb their hair, change their clothes, and even make them talk.
   d _ _ _ _

g You might find it difficult to hear after one of these, especially if you stand near the front.
   r _ _ _ c _ _ _ _ _ _

h If you can't afford to buy a lot of it, you can get some silver or gold and make it yourself.
   j _ _ _ _ _ _ _ _

i Actors sing and dance, and often wear colourful costumes.
   m _ _ _ _ _ _

j Children buy and sell these in the playground at school; adults might prefer to use the Internet!
   t _ _ _ _ _ _ c _ _ _ _

k Some people buy and collect things connected with Princess Diana: cups and plates, key rings, books, etc.
   m _ _ _ _ _ _ _ _ _ _

Vocabulary booster: -ed and -ing adjectives

8

a Match one of the adjectives with a face.

bored	interested	~~surprised~~	tired	relaxed
excited	frightened	worried		

1 _surprised_

2 _____

3 _____

4 _____

5 _____

6 _____

7 _____

8 _____

b **T11.3** Listen and check. Practise saying the words.

c How do you feel when:

1 you listen to classical music? _____
2 you watch a football match on TV? _____
3 you see a spider? _____
4 your best friend doesn't phone you for a few days? _____
5 you stay up after 2 a.m.? _____
6 someone talks to you about cars? _____

> **LOOK!**
>
> Some adjectives have both -ed and -ing forms, for example: bored / boring.
>
> The -ing form describes the way something is.
> The -ed form describes the way it makes you feel.

d Circle the best form, -ed or -ing.

1 Driving for a long time can be *tired* / *tiring*.
2 A long walk in the park can be *relaxed* / *relaxing*.
3 If you have nothing to do, you may be *bored* / *boring*.
4 A piece of news can be *surprised* / *surprising*.
5 You can be *interested* / *interesting* in football.
6 Going for a swim can be *relaxed* / *relaxing*.
7 A film can be *excited* / *exciting*.
8 People can be *worried* / *worrying* about losing their job.
9 Hard work can make you *tired* / *tiring*.
10 Some people find the dark *frightened* / *frightening*.
11 You might be *shocked* / *shocking* if you get a very big phone bill.
12 Some English grammar rules are *confused* / *confusing*.

Wordspot
like

9 a Complete the sentences with a phrase with *like*.

1 A: Is your food OK?

B: Oh yes, it _____ the risotto my mother used to make. Delicious!

2 A: Do you _____ going for a walk?

B: Not really. I think it's going to rain.

3 A: You're lucky – you never put on weight.

B: I know – I can eat _____ and I don't get fat!

4 A: You've got a lot of bags there – I'll carry some for you, if _____ .

B: Oh thank you, that's very kind.

5 A: I met our new neighbours yesterday.

B: Oh yes – _____ ?

A: They seem very friendly.

6 A: Look at that man over there – don't you think he _____ Robert de Niro?

B: Not really – he's too young.

7 A: What's this dress made of? It _____ silk – so soft.

B: It is silk, actually. It's a good price, isn't it?

8 A: I'm collecting money for a leaving present for Sasha. _____ to give something?

B: Oh yes, of course. Here's $10.

9 A: Patrick's arriving on Saturday and he's got nowhere to stay.

B: Tell him he can stay with us, if _____ . We've got lots of room.

10 A: So this is a traditional recipe for fruit cake?

B: Yes, we always make it _____ in our family.

b **T11.4** Listen and check.

Spelling
Words ending with *-ion*

10 a All these verbs have a noun form ending with *-ion*. Write the nouns.

1 collect   *collection*

2 decide   _____

3 describe   _____

4 discuss   _____

5 educate   _____

6 explain   _____

7 invite   _____

8 permit   _____

9 prepare   _____

10 pronounce   _____

b Complete these *-ion* words.

1 fa _ _ ion   6 rela _ ionship

2 ambi _ ion   7 tradi _ ional

3 obse _ _ ion   8 revi _ ion

4 conversa _ ion   9 na _ ionality

5 profe _ _ ional

Pronunciation
Words ending with *-ion*

11 a **T11.5** Listen to the pronunciation of these *-ion* words. Is the *-ion* syllable strong or weak? Underline the stressed syllable in each word.

1 col<u>lec</u>tion   7 permission

2 education   8 traditional

3 discussion   9 occasion

4 relationship   10 revision

5 decision   11 fashion

6 conversation   12 nationality

b Listen again and practise saying the words. Pay attention to the stress, and to the weak pronunciation of the *-ion* syllable.

Improve your writing
Replying to invitations

12 a Georgina is from Ireland. She is studying Italian in Rome. Read three invitations that she received while she was there and match them to her replies. Write the names in the gaps.

A

Hi Georgina

We're going for a picnic in the park after class today. Do you want to come? Bring something to eat and drink, and meet us in the reception area at 4 p.m.

See you

Frank and Lottie

B

from: christina112@optusnet.com
to: georgi-g@yahoo.com

Dear Georgina
How are you? I know I haven't been in touch for a while, but I've been so busy, and guess what? Marc and I are engaged! We are going to get married next year some time, but we're having an engagement party on Saturday 21st June, from 6–11 pm. I do hope you can come: it's at my parent's house in Dublin (you remember how to get there, don't you?).
Really looking forward to seeing you again.
Christina

C

Via Spiga 444 / 13 B
Roma
4.6.05

Dear Georgina,
I don't know if you will remember me: my name is Lucia Conti, and I was a friend of your mother's at university. My husband and I stayed at your house for a few days several years ago, when we were on holiday.
Anyway, I heard that you were studying here, and I was wondering if you would like to come and stay with us for the weekend, maybe next weekend or the one after that? We would love to see you, and I know what it is like to be away from home in a different country. You would also be able to try some authentic home-cooked Italian food – my husband is a great cook!
I'm looking forward to seeing you – just let me know when you can come and we will pick you up.
Best wishes,

Lucia Conti

1

Dear _____
First of all, congratulations! I am very happy for you. However, I'm afraid I won't be able to come to your engagement party because I am in Rome, studying Italian, until the end of August. What a shame! Have a wonderful time, and I hope to see you when I get back.
All the best
Georgina

2

Dear _____
Thank you very much for inviting me to stay, it was so kind of you. I'd love to come, but next weekend I am going on an excursion with the school, so the one after that would be best for me.
I'm looking forward to trying your husband's cooking.
Best wishes
Georgina

3

Dear _____
That sounds great. I'll get some cola, and some bread and cheese.
See you at 4
Georgina

b Which invitation does Georgina refuse? Why?

c Without looking back at the replies, write complete phrases for accepting and refusing invitations. Then look back and check.

1 That / sound / great

_____

2 Thank you very much / invite / me / stay, it / so kind / you

_____

3 I / afraid / I / be able / come / your party

_____

4 I / love / come, but I / go / on an excursion

_____

5 I / look / forward / try / your husband's cooking

_____

6 What / shame!

_____

d Imagine that you have received one of the following invitations. Write a reply, accepting or refusing the invitation.

- an invitation to your cousin's wedding
- an invitation to lunch with some elderly relatives
- an invitation to go and stay with some friends in a house by the beach

Passive forms
Identifying passive forms

1 Rock star Bob Goldhart has been one of the USA's favourite rock stars for more than thirty years. Here are the titles of some of his songs. Write P next to the song titles which include passive forms and A next to the songs which include active forms.

a 'Am I Forgiven?' _P_

b 'I was Made to Love You' _____

c 'You Told Me You Loved Me (And That was a Lie)' _____

d 'Rock 'n' Roll will Never Die' _____

e 'My Heart was Stolen (By a Disco Queen)' _____

f 'The Man who Bought the World' _____

g 'My Heart is Made of Glass' _____

h 'It Wasn't Easy (But I did it Anyway)' _____

i 'Tonight is the Most Beautiful Night' _____

j 'I Am Adored (By all the World)' _____

Present simple passive

2 Put the verb in brackets into the Present simple passive.

a About 300,000,000 photocopies _are made_____ (make) in Europe every day.

b The word 'the' _____ (use) 63,924 times in the Bible.

c 4,250 postmen _____ (bite) by British dogs every year.

d 3,822 cars _____ (steal) in the United States every day.

e 112 different languages _____ (speak) in the Russian Federation.

f Seventy-one percent of the world _____ (cover) by water.

g In a normal year, five people _____ (kill) by lightning in England and Wales.

h 2.4 litres of water _____ (lose) by the human body every day.

Questions

3 Put the words in the correct order to make questions and find the answers in the box below.

to see in the dark	~~in supermarkets and pharmacies~~
to stop it melting	water, sugar and a secret ingredient
to mobile phones	in Brazil and Portugal
over your eyes	with 'be' and the past participle

a is / sold / Where / shampoo

Where is shampoo sold?

In supermarkets and pharmacies.

b spoken / Portuguese / is / Where

_____ ?

_____

c made / cola / What / of / is

_____ ?

_____

d are / sent / Where / text messages

_____ ?

_____

e freezer / is / Why / ice cream / a / kept / in

_____ ?

_____

f used / What / for / torch / a / is

_____ ?

_____

g sunglasses / worn / usually / are / Where

_____ ?

_____

h is / passive / made / the / How

_____ ?

_____

Active or passive?

4 Tick (✓) the correct sentence.

1 a Twenty people arrested at the demonstration. ☐

   b Twenty people were arrested at the demonstration. ☑

2 a Mona Lisa painted Leonardo da Vinci. ☐

   b Mona Lisa was painted by Leonardo da Vinci. ☐

3 a Magellan sailed around the world about 500 years ago. ☐

   b Magellan was sailed around the world about 500 years ago. ☐

4 a Steven Spielberg directed the film *Schindler's List*. ☐

   b Steven Spielberg was directed the film *Schindler's List*. ☐

5 a *Romeo and Juliet* wrote William Shakespeare. ☐

   b *Romeo and Juliet* was written by William Shakespeare. ☐

6 a Unfortunately, our dog was killed in a road accident. ☐

   b Unfortunately, our dog killed in a road accident. ☐

7 a The cathedral in our town built about 400 years ago. ☐

   b The cathedral in our town was built about 400 years ago. ☐

8 a All her clothes are made in Italy. ☐

   b All her clothes made in Italy. ☐

Past simple passive

5 Complete the biography of the designer Gianni Versace by putting the verbs in brackets into the Past simple passive.

Designer
of
the Decade

Italian Gianni Versace was one of the best-known fashion designers of the twentieth century.

Sometimes his clothes (a) *were criticised* (criticise), but they (b) _____ (buy) by the rich and famous – particularly people from the worlds of pop music and film.

Versace came from Calabria, in the south of Italy, where his mother was a dressmaker. He moved to the northern city of Milan in the 1970s, and his first collection (c) _____ (launch) in 1978.

Soon, his brother Santo and his sister Donatella (d) _____ (give) jobs in the growing Versace empire. He bought homes in Milan, Paris, New York and Miami, which (e) _____ (fill) with works of art from all over the world.

In 1994, the English actress Elizabeth Hurley wore a Versace dress on the first night of the film *Four Weddings and a Funeral* in London. The simple black dress which (f) _____ (hold) together by a few safety pins was a sensation. The next day, the photos (g) _____ (see) all over the world and from that moment the name Versace (h) _____ (know) everywhere.

His clothes (i) _____ (wear) by superstars such as Elton John, Madonna, Courtney Love, Princess Diana and the supermodel Naomi Campbell.

Versace (j) _____ (murder) on 15 July 1997 outside his home in Miami Beach. His memorial service in Milan Cathedral (k) _____ (attend) by 2,000 people: millions watched on television as a tearful Elton John (l) _____ (comfort) by Princess Diana – who herself died tragically just a few weeks later.

Questions

6 a Use the prompts to make questions and find the answers on pages 108 and 171 of the Students' Book.

1 Who / shampoo / develop / by
   Who was shampoo developed by?
   John Breck

2 Who / jeans / design / by
   _____
   _____ ?
   _____

3 Why / sunglasses / wear / by Chinese judges
   _____
   _____ ?
   _____

4 Who / Chanel No. 5 / introduce by
   _____
   _____ ?
   _____

5 When / first DVD player / manufacture
   _____
   _____ ?
   _____

6 When / disposable razor / invent
   _____
   _____ ?
   _____

7 How / 'Nike' / pronounce
   _____
   _____ ?
   _____

8 Where / Nike tick / recognise
   _____
   _____ ?
   _____

b 〔T12.1〕 Listen and check.

Listen and read

7 a **T12.2** Listen to and read the text *Diamonds are Forever*.

Diamonds are forever

'Diamonds,' sang Marilyn Monroe in the film *Gentlemen Prefer Blondes*, 'are a girl's best friend.' You might not agree, but we can be sure of this: diamonds are not only the hardest substance in the world, they are also the most expensive. A single diamond cost $16.5 million when it was sold in Geneva in 1995!

Diamonds are found in a number of countries including Australia, South Africa and Brazil. In fact, there are two types of diamond; colourless diamonds (about 25% of those found) are the hardest and are often made into jewels. Black diamonds – the remaining 75% – are usually used by industry. Industrial diamonds are also produced artificially.

The largest diamond in history is the Cullinan diamond. It weighed 620g and was mined in South Africa in 1905. It was bought by the Transvaal government for £150,000, and then it was presented to the King of England, Edward VII. The diamond was cut into smaller jewels, which are now part of the British Crown Jewels, which belong to the Queen of England and are kept in the Tower of London.

Diamonds are also used for decoration. Between 1885 and 1917, the Russian jeweller Peter Carl Fabergé made a number of decorated Easter eggs for the tsars and their families. The most valuable of them is decorated with more than 3,000 diamonds. It was sold at Christie's, Geneva for $5.5 million.

b Using the information in the text, complete the sentences below with either the active or the passive form of the verb.

1 Marilyn Monroe / sing / *Diamonds are a Girl's Best Friend*

   Marilyn Monroe sang 'Diamonds are a Girl's Best Friend'.

2 A $16.5 million diamond / sell / in Geneva / in 1995

   _____

3 Diamonds / find / in many countries, including South Africa and Brazil

   _____
   _____

4 Colourless diamonds / make / into jewels

   _____

5 Black diamonds / use / in industry

   _____

6 The Transvaal government / give / the Cullinan diamond to King Edward VII

   _____
   _____

7 The diamond / cut / into smaller diamonds

   _____
   _____

8 Peter Fabergé / make / egg which / sell / for $5.5 million at Christie's.

   _____
   _____

Vocabulary
Everyday objects

8 See how many questions you can answer, then look at page 106 of the Students' Book to check.

a Which **c** do you use to keep your hair tidy?

c _omb_____

b Which **c c** can you use instead of cash to buy things? c_____ c_____

c Which **d l** do you need if you want to hire a car?

d_____ l_____

d Which **i c** can you use to prove your age?

i_____ c_____

e Which **k** do you need to start your car? k_____

f Which **m p** can you use to call, send texts, or even take photos? **m**_____ **p**_____

g Which **p** do you put on a cut or scratch? **p**_____

h Which **r** is used to take away hair? **r**_____

i Which **s f** is also used to help a **r** to take away hair? s_____ f_____

j Which **u** do you put up in the rain? **u**_____

Spelling / Pronunciation
Silent 'g' and 'gh'

9 a **T12.3** Listen to these words.

> LOOK!
> In the word *design*, the g is silent.
> In the word *sunglasses*, it is pronounced as /g/.
> In the word *night*, the gh is silent.
> In the word *cough*, it is pronounced as /f/.

b How are 'g' and 'gh' pronounced in these words? Write *silent*, /g/ or /f/ by each word.

1 li**gh**ter   _silent_____

2 lau**gh**   _____

3 bou**gh**t   _____

4 si**g**n   _____

5 enou**gh**   _____

6 si**g**nature   _____

7 hei**gh**t   _____

8 green**g**rocer   _____

c **T12.4** Listen and check your pronunciation.

Real life
Making suggestions

10 Correct the mistake in each conversation.

a A: Shall I to come and pick you up at the station?

B: Yes, that would be great.

b A: There's nothing on TV – do you want to go out somewhere?

B: OK, let go to that new café opposite the cinema.

c A: I'm so tired, and I really don't feel well.

B: Well, why don't you take the rest of the day off.

A: Yes, maybe I do that.

d A: It's my wife's birthday on Friday and I don't know what to do to celebrate.

B: You take her to a concert, then go for dinner afterwards.

A: Mm, good idea.

e A: I've got to get Melissa a present for looking after my cat.

B: Well, what about get her a box of chocolates?

f A: Come on: why we don't go down to the river for a walk?

B: Oh no, it's much too cold.

g A: I really don't know what to wear to Carl and Linda's wedding.

B: You've got lots of nice clothes: how is this suit?

A: Hm, I don't know …

Vocabulary booster
Outdoor equipment

11   a   Label the picture with words from the box.

> a tent   some matches   a sleeping bag   a tin opener   a blanket
> some insect repellent   a coolbox   a thermos flask   a penknife   a torch
> a fishing rod   a back pack   a portable stove   a waterproof jacket

b   Which of the items can you use:

- when you prepare food? _____
- to keep you warm and/or dry? _____
- to carry things? _____
- when you need a light? _____

Present perfect continuous

1 Write one sentence using the Present perfect continuous for each pair of pictures.

a   *She has been working in the office for two hours.* (work)

b _____ (rain)

c _____ (play tennis)

d _____ (walk)

Time phrases with *for* and *since*

2 Write *for* or *since* next to these time phrases.

a   *for*_____ a week
b   *since*_____ 1990
c   _____ twenty minutes
d   _____ he was born
e   _____ Thursday
f   _____ then
g   _____ last week
h   _____ nine o'clock
i   _____ this morning
j   _____ you left school
k   _____ six months
l   _____ an hour
m   _____ twenty years

Present perfect with *for* and *since*

3 **a** **Choose one of the phrases from Exercise 2 to complete each sentence in a logical way.**

1   Today's the last day of our holiday: we've been here *for a week*_____ .
2   She left home two days ago, and no one has seen her _____ .
3   You probably haven't studied mathematics _____ .
4   I'm not surprised you're hungry – you haven't eaten _____ .
5   The American singer Stevie Wonder has been blind _____ .
6   Germany has been re-united _____ .
7   Excuse me, waitress. Is our meal coming? We've been waiting _____ !
8   I've been driving _____ and I've never had an accident!

b **T13.1** **Listen and check.**

4 Read the text below. Use the prompts to write questions, and write answers with *for* or *since*.

Success from abroad

Thomas Eckhardt: Thomas came to London from Germany almost four years ago. After doing a course in theatre costume design, he began working at the National Theatre in London a year ago. 'I really enjoy designing clothes, and I've always loved the theatre, so this job is absolutely perfect for me,' he says. 'I started work on a new production of *Romeo and Juliet* two weeks ago and I'm really excited about it.'

Bianca and Richard Jones: Bianca Jones is originally from Lima, in Peru. She came to England in 1997, and a year later she got married. For the last two years she has been manager of *La Finca* restaurant with her English husband, Richard. 'We were London's only Peruvian restaurant. It's been so successful that last week we opened a new restaurant – *La Finca II.*'

Kerry Paterson: When Kerry first came to England from Australia in 2000 she was a backpacker, travelling round Europe. She came back three years later and started working as a swimming coach about a year after that. Nowadays, she has a second, part-time job – playing in a jazz band. 'About a month ago, a friend heard that I could play the piano, and asked me to join his band. We play every weekend in local cafés and restaurants.'

a How long / Thomas / live / in England?
   How long has Thomas been living in England?
   for four years

b How long / he / work / at the National Theatre?
   _____ ?
   _____

c How long / he / work / on *Romeo and Juliet*?
   _____ ?
   _____

d How long / Bianca / live / in England?
   _____ ?
   _____

e How long / she / work / at *La Finca*?
   _____ ?
   _____

f How long / *La Finca II* / operate?
   _____ ?
   _____

g How long / Kerry / live / in England?
   _____ ?
   _____

h How long / she / work / as a swimming coach?
   _____ ?
   _____

i How long / she / play / in a jazz band?
   _____ ?
   _____

Present perfect continuous and Present perfect simple
Stative verbs

5 Read the Look! box on page 24 of your Workbook again. Five of the sentences below should be in the Present perfect simple. Find them and correct them.

a I've been working for about three hours. ✓
b I've been having this watch for over twenty years.
c The President has been talking for nearly an hour.
d How long have you been waiting?
e I've been liking chocolate for years.
f Have you been knowing Sylvia for a long time?
g She's been reading that book for weeks.
h I haven't been seeing Michael for years and years.
i I've been hating spinach since I was a child.
j Caroline has been staying with her grandmother for the last two weeks.

b – I've had this watch for over
twenty years.
_____
_____
_____
_____
_____
_____
_____
_____
_____
_____
_____
_____

Reading

6 a These job advertisements all come from the same website: *jobsearch.com*, which advertises jobs for young people all over the world. Read the advertisements and complete the table.

	The job	Where it is	Dates
1			
2			
3			
4			

Address: www.jobsearch.com

jobsearch.com

Jobs for students, recent graduates and people looking for adventure

1

The Chaweng Beach Center, Samui
Management Trainee

Job Location: Samui Island, Suratthani, Thailand

Job Description: We are looking for an English-speaking person to work as a Management Trainee at the Chaweng Beach Center in Samui, Thailand. If you speak fluent English and want to work in the hotel and tourism business, why not apply for this job?

The working period will be from July to September. Monthly salary of 6,000 baht; your accommodation and meals are free. Transportation and visa will be your responsibility. The hotel will arrange a work permit for you. For more information, please contact:

Training Manager
The Chaweng Beach Center
63/3 Moo 5, Borpud
Koh Samui, Chaweng Beach
Suratthani, Thailand 82340
Phone: 66 77 231504
Fax: 66 77 231528
e-mail: chawenres@samart.co.th
www.centralbeachresorts.com

2

Hotel Waitress

Job Location: Island of Sark, Guernsey, Channel Islands

Region: UK

Job Description: Hotel Beauchamp, situated on the beautiful, small island of Sark in the Channel Islands, requires waitress from end of May until mid-September. 16-room private hotel with restaurant. Good salary and working conditions, live-in accommodation at the hotel. Experience not essential.

Contact: Mr & Mrs M. Robinson

Hotel Beauchamp, Sark
Via Guernsey, Channel Islands GY9 OSF
Phone: 01481 238046
Fax: 01481 238469
e-mail: hotbe@island-of-sark.co.uk

next ▶

b Now read the advertisements again and complete the table below.

	You need to …	Salary
1	speak fluent English	
2		
3		
4		

Back **Forward** **Stop** **Refresh** **Home** **Favorites** **History** **Search** **AutoFill** **Larger** **Smaller** **Print** **Mail** **Preferences**

Address: www.jobsearch.com

jobsearch.com

Jobs for students, recent graduates and people looking for adventure

3

Chamont Hot-Air Balloon Ground Crew

Job Location:	Europe
Region:	France, Switzerland, Austria, Italy
Job Description:	The Chamont Balloon Adventures team travels to France, Italy, Switzerland, Austria, the Czech Republic and Turkey, from May through October and the Swiss Alps, in January through February. Since 1977, we have offered hot-air balloon flights to an international clientele.
	To be a ground assistant, you must be fit, with a cheerful personality: knowledge of spoken French, Italian and/or German is an advantage. Driving licence essential.
	Accommodation and food included, as well as a small salary. To apply send CV, ID photo and photocopy of driving licence.
	We are currently hiring for our summer season (24 May through 30 October).
Contact:	Michel Chamont
	Chamont Balloon Adventures Château de Labourde Dijon, FRANCE 21200 e-mail: mchamont@compuserve.com

4

Peking Garden

Chef - for Chinese Takeaway

Job Location:	Tallinn, Estonia.
Job Description:	Qualified chef needed for period of approximately six months in busy Chinese takeaway restaurant in Tallinn, Estonia. Salary $800–1000 per month. Please contact us by e-mail.
Contact:	Peking Garden Chinese Restaurant
	Pronksi 8-45 Tallinn, Estonia 10421 Phone: (372) 25023896 FAX: (372) 26184588 e-mail: peking@evr.ee

back

Vocabulary
Personal characteristics

7 Use the clues to complete the grid below. The words all come from page 00 of the Students' Book.

a | | | | I | | | | | |
b | | | | M | | | | | |
c | | | | A | | | | | |
d | | | | G | | | | | |
e | | | | I | | | | | |
f | | | | N | | | | | |
g | | | | A | | | | | |
h | | | | T | | | | | |
i | | | | I | | | | | |
j | | | | O | | | | | |
k | | | | N | | | | | |

a   If you lose this, you may not finish your work or achieve you goals. (10 letters)
b   You are this if you want something very much and you work very hard to get it. (9 letters)
c   Some singers have a lot of natural _____ , others have to practise and study hard. (6 letters)
d   If you are well-_____ , you know where everything is, and you make good use of your time. (9 letters)
e   You need a lot of self-_____ if you want to follow a diet and lose weight. (10 letters)
f   You are this if you tell the truth and do not steal things. (6 letters)
g   You are this if you try to understand other people's problems and help them. (11 letters)
h   Someone who is a good _____ is patient and pays attention to what the other person is saying. (8 letters)
i   Most people would rather have an _____ pilot than someone who has never flown a plane before! (11 letters)
j   Completely (7 letters)
k   This will not help you to pass exams or get a good job. (8 letters)

Wordspot
how

8 a Complete the questions with a phrase with *how*. Then match the questions to the answers a–k.

1   _____ your sister feeling after her operation?
2   Mr Takamoto? George Harvey. _____ ?
3   I'm hungry. _____ stopping at that cafe for some lunch?
4   _____ people have you invited to the wedding?
5   Does anyone know _____ it is to the nearest petrol station?
6   _____ pronounce this word? Is it /ei/ or /ai/?
7   What a beautiful building. Do you know _____ it is?
8   _____ have you had that ring? I've never seen it before.
9   I love your new haircut. _____ did you pay for it?
10 _____ does it take to get to the coast from here?
11 Hello Frankie. Haven't you grown! _____ are you now?
12 _____ tortilla? Eggs, potatoes, and what else?

a   I don't think there's one for at least 50 km.
b   I'm 1.21m.
c   Nothing. My brother did it – he's doing a hairdressing course.
d   She's out of hospital, but she's still very tired.
e   Onions, I think. Haven't you got a cookery book?
f   I'm not sure. At least 100 years old, I'd say.
g   Only about twenty minutes by car.
h   How do you do? I'm pleased to meet you.
i   Not many. About thirty so far.
j   I've had it for years – I don't wear it very often.
k   I don't know. Why don't you ask the teacher?
l   Good idea. Breakfast was ages ago!

b **T13.2** Listen and check.

Pronunciation
Some 'hard to pronounce' words

9 a Look at the words below. Is the sound in bold pronounced the same as the word in A or B?

	A	B
lawyer	how	✓ four
disc**i**pline	✓ sit	ship
h**o**nest	not	home
p**a**tient	**pa**n	**pai**nting
psych**ia**trist	here	fire
awful	more	now
he**a**lth	fell	feel
ar**chi**tect	**chi**ldren	heada**che**

b **T13.3** Listen and check. Practise saying both words.

Improve your writing
Error correction (1)

10 a Read the letter below. Find:

1 five punctuation mistakes (full stops, capital letters, etc.).
2 three layout mistakes (where things are on the page).
3 four spelling mistakes.
4 two mistakes of politeness.

b Write out the letter in full, correcting all the mistakes.

374 Upper Road
Islington
London
N1 2XG

Tel. 020 7359 1410

March 26th 2001

hello Sir!

    I am writeing to apply for a job as a member of your chamont balloon adventures ground crew. I inclose a CV, ID photo and photocopy of my driving licence as requested. I am avalable to start work immediatly.

Thanks a lot

    Jean Guinard.

Michael Chamont
Chamont Balloon Adventures
Château de Labourde
Dijon
FRANCE 21200

MODULE 14

Past perfect

1 **a** Put the verbs in brackets into the Past perfect to complete the sentences below.

1   Nadia said she was very sorry for what she
_had done_____ (do).

2   When Sam
_____ (pay)
the bill, we left the restaurant and went home.

3   It wasn't surprising that she was tired: she

_____
(not / sleep) for two days.

4   The children were very excited because they

_____
(not / see) a tiger before.

5   The road was blocked because a lorry _____
(break down).

6   During the afternoon, David lost all the money he
_____ (win)
in the morning.

7   My mother felt very nervous on the plane because she

_____
(not / fly) before.

8   When the police arrived to arrest him, Thompson

_____
(leave).

b **T14.1** Listen and check. Practise saying the sentences.

Past perfect and Past simple

2 Complete the text about Justine Klaus with the correct form of the verb in brackets: Past simple or Past perfect.

When Swiss millionairess Justine Klaus (a) _died_ (die) in Geneva at the age of seventy-nine, most of her family (b) _____ (come) to hear the details of her will, hoping the old lady (c) _____ (remember) them. Instead they (d) _____ (get) a real shock. Justine (e) _____ (live) alone for many years, and most of her family (f) _____ (not/see) her for several years. Her relatives (g) _____ (be) amazed when they (h) _____ (hear) that the old lady (i) _____ (leave) £370,000 to her favourite house plant! Justine said that for all those years the plant (j) _____ (be) her best and only friend. In contrast, her family only (k) _____ (receive) £100 each.

Irregular past forms

3 Circle the correct form of the verb to complete the sentences.

a   The show had already *began* / *begun* when we got to the stadium.

b   It was a marvellous show, and Maria *sang* / *sung* beautifully.

c   I was very tired because I had *drove* / *driven* all the way from Edinburgh to London.

d   While I was swimming in the sea, someone *stolen* / *stole* my clothes.

e   When she died in 1999, the novelist Iris Murdoch had *wrote* / *written* twenty-seven novels.

f   The X-rays showed that Laurence had *broke* / *broken* his leg.

g   I had never *saw* / *seen* anything so beautiful in my whole life.

h   When we got home, the children had *fell* / *fallen* asleep in the car.

i   I didn't think you *knew* / *known* about the company's money problems.

j   I couldn't try any of the cake, because Alice had *took* / *taken* the last piece.

Past time words: *already, just, never ... before*

4 Put the words in the correct order to make sentences.

a been / before / abroad / had / Carla / never

Carla had never been abroad before.

b When / closed / shop / I / there / just / the / got / had

_____

c you / met / I / already / had / brother / thought / my

_____

d doorbell / I / when / had / finished / just / the / rang / dinner

_____

e before / way / knew / We / because / been / had / the / there / we

_____

f the / got / left / plane / airport / When / had / we / to / already / the

_____

5 Rewrite the sentences using *already*, *just* or *never ... before*.

a Martha had finished the report a short time before Mr Harris asked for it.

Martha had just finished the report when

Mr Harris asked for it.

b It was the first time I had been skiing.

_____

_____

c I wanted to speak to Philip, but he had gone home earlier than I expected.

_____

_____

d Eating frogs' legs was a new experience for Sally.

_____

_____

e My friends had ordered their food some time before I got to the restaurant.

_____

_____

f I had left the house a few seconds before it started to rain.

_____

_____

Past time words: Past perfect or Present perfect?

6 Tick (✓) the correct ending for each of these sentences.

a That meal we had last night was delicious.
1 I've never tried Lebanese food before.
2 I'd never tried Lebanese food before. ✓

b I didn't need to tell Jake to do his homework because
1 he'd already done it.
2 he's already done it.

c Who's that girl talking to Sophie?
1 I've never seen her before.
2 I'd never seen her before.

d Sorry I didn't answer the phone:
1 I've just gone to bed when you rang.
2 I'd just gone to bed when you rang.

e 'You look happy.'
1 'I've just won £2000 in the lottery!'
2 'I'd just won £2000 in the lottery!'

f You can't go in now, madam.
1 The concert has already started.
2 The concert had already started.

Vocabulary
Money

7 Complete the gaps to make sentences which have the same meaning.

1 The computer was too expensive for me to buy.
  I _couldn't afford_ the computer.

2 Philip borrowed £1,000 from his friend Gill.
  Gill _____ £1,000 to her friend _____ .

3 In this job, your salary will be £30,000 a year.
  In this job, you will _____ £30,000 a year.

4 I forgot that I borrowed £10 from Joseph.
  I haven't _____ the £20 that I borrowed from Joseph yet.

5 I was very disappointed by the holiday. It wasn't a good way to spend my money.
  I was very disappointed by the holiday. It was a _____ money.

6 In the TV Programme *Millionaire* you can receive up to £1 million by answering simple questions.
  In the TV Programme *Millionaire* you can _____ up to £1 million by answering simple questions.

7 I'm going to spend less money so I can buy a motorbike.
  I'm going to _____ money to buy a motorbike.

8 When the company closed, all the investors' money disappeared.
  When the company closed, the investors _____ all their money.

Prepositions

8 Complete the gaps with the correct preposition.

a I tried to borrow some money ___from___ my parents, but they said no.

b When I have enough money _____ the bank, I'll retire.

c Thomas spends about £150 a month _____ clothes.

d Can I change this money _____ US dollars, please?

e Last year the company made a profit _____ £200,000.

f I'm afraid you can't pay _____ credit card in this restaurant: they only accept cash.

g 'How would you like to pay, madam?' 'I'll pay _____ cash.'

h Can you wait a minute? I need to get some money _____ _____ the bank.

i Be careful if you lend money _____ Richard. He never pays it back.

j Mick sold his laptop to Patrick _____ £500.

Vocabulary booster: shopping

9
a **T14.2** Answer the quiz questions. Then listen and check.

1	A period of time when a shop sells things at lower prices than usual is: *a a sale.* *b a reduction.*
2	If you buy something for a good price, it is: *a a discount.* *b a bargain.*
3	If you are looking in shop windows but not intending to buy anything, you are: *a window buying.* *b window shopping.*
4	If you put on some clothes in a shop to see if they are the right size, you: *a try them on.* *b try them out.*
5	When you pay for something, the shop assistant gives you: *a a receipt.* *b a ticket.*
6	If something is faulty and you take it back to the shop, you can ask for: *a a payback.* *b a refund.*
7	A big shop which sells different types of goods such as clothes, furniture, stationery, etc., is: *a a shopping mall.* *b a department store.*
8	A boutique is a small shop which sells: *a food.* *b clothes.*
9	If you buy something which is a present for someone, you can ask the assistant to: *a cover it.* *b wrap it.*
10	The crime of stealing things from shops is called: *a shoplifting.* *b shoptaking.*

b Complete the sentences with words from part a.

1 I took the shoes back to the shop but they wouldn't give me a _____ because I'd lost my _____ .

2 While I was shopping in the supermarket yesterday, a woman was arrested for _____ .

3 David Jones are having a _____ this week. I bought this coat for £30: a real _____ .

4 I haven't got time to _____ this shirt _____ . I hope it's the right size.

5 A good choice. Your niece will love it, madam. Would you like me to _____ for you?

6 When we were in California we went _____ in Rodeo Drive where clothes were incredibly expensive.

Wordspot
make

10
Complete the sentences with the correct form of *make* and a word from the box.

a mistake	laugh	a decision	some sandwiches
~~sad~~	a noise	stay	£15	a speech	feel

a It really ____*makes*____ me ____*sad*____ when I see all those homeless people on the streets.

b Ssh! Don't _____ – we shouldn't be here.

c I hope I don't have to _____ at the wedding: I hate public speaking.

d Josh's mum and dad _____ him _____ at home all weekend because he got such bad grades at school.

e I've _____ to eat on the journey.

f Tom _____ by selling some of his old play station games to his friends at school.

g Sorry, I _____ . It's £15, not £20.

h What are you going to do about the problems in the factory? Have you _____ yet?

i Let's invite Harry. He's got a lot to say and he always _____ everyone _____ .

j You really think I was wrong to say that? Now you're _____ me _____ guilty.

Pronunciation
The sounds /eɪ/ and /e/

11
a **T14.3** Listen to the /eɪ/ and /e/ sounds in the following words.

/e/ lend bread spend
/eɪ/ break day make

b Look at the sentences. Mark the /eɪ/ and /e/ sounds.

1 I've made about ten phone calls today.
 /eɪ/   /e/   /eɪ/

2 They wasted all the money we gave them.

_____

3 Have you read the book I lent you, by the way?

_____

4 She said she'd pay me back at the end of April.

_____

5 Jane made a terrible mistake.

_____

c **T14.4** Listen and check. Practise saying the sentences.

Listen and read

12 **a** Complete the text using the phrases in the box.

> But they weren't used in Europe   a thing of the past   ~~How much money~~
> began to appear   a £10 bank note   about 2,700 years ago
> pieces of paper   as people became rich

(1)__How much money__ have you got with you today? How
many coins? How many notes? Why is money so important anyway?
If you think about it, coins are just discs of metal, and bank notes are
just (2)_____ . Money is only money if we agree
that it's worth something! Nowadays, governments print bank notes
and guarantee their value. As well as the Queen's head, all British
bank notes carry the words: *I promise to pay the bearer on demand the
sum of ...* Originally that meant that it was possible for you to take
(3)_____ to the Bank of England and ask for £10
of gold in return.

   Over the years, money has taken many forms. In China people
used precious shells; hundreds of years later the Vikings in Northern
Europe used jewellery, and the people of ancient Tibet once used
blocks of dried tea! People from ancient Lydia (Turkey) were the first
to make coins, (4)_____ . The coins were made
from electrum, a mixture of gold and silver. It wasn't until the
eleventh century that paper bank notes (5)_____
in China. (6)_____ until the Middle Ages when
traders and bankers used 'bills of exchange' instead of cash. The
modern industries of banking and insurance soon followed
(7)_____ through trade between East and West.

   With the growth of the 'virtual economy', some people predict
that, within twenty years, coins and notes will be
(8)_____ : we will all use 'smart cards' to buy
things. No more worries about losing your wallet or purse ... but what
if you lose the card?

b [T14.5] Listen and check.

c Answer the questions below about the text.

1 Can you really change a £10 note for £10 of gold at the Bank of England?

_____

2 Can you exchange dollar bills for gold in the USA?

_____

3 What did people use for money in:

a) Ancient China? _____

b) Viking Europe? _____

c) Ancient Tibet? _____

4 Who made the first coins? When?

_____

_____

5 When did the first bank notes appear? Where?

_____

_____

6 When did bank notes first appear in Europe?

_____

7 What do some people predict will replace money?

_____

Real life
Dealing with money

13 Match the beginnings of the sentences in A with the endings in B and write them in the correct places in the dialogues below.

A	B
I'd like to	included?
Can I have	ties?
What's the exchange	to the pound.
Is service	open a bank account.
Can I pay	one.
It's 2.4 dollars	the bill please?
I'll take this	do I need?
If I could just	by credit card?
How much are these	rate for Australian dollars?
What documents	see your passport.

a
  A: Can I change some money here?
  B: Yes, certainly.
  A: (1) _What's the exchange rate for Australian_ _dollars?_
  B: (2) _____
  A: OK, well I've got £300 pounds here.
  B: Right. (3) _____

b
  A: (1) _____ ?
  B: One moment – here you are.
  A: Thank you. (2) _____ ?
  B: Yes, we take Visa or Mastercard, but not American Express.
  A: That's fine. Oh, and (3) _____ ?
  B: No, it isn't.

c
  A: Can I help you?
  B: Yes – (1) _____ ?
  A: The blue one's £25 and the red and white one is silk – that's £130.
  B: I see. Well, (2) _____

d
  A: (1) _____
  B: Right, well you need to fill in this form and bring the necessary documents ...
  A: Oh. (2) _____ ?
  B: Just your passport, and something with your address on it.

Improve your writing
Paying online

14 Michael Sheppard is booking a flight on the Internet, using his credit card.

- His address is: 144 Acorn Avenue, Toronto, Canada M3V 4B1.
- His phone number is: (416) 43789103

Look at the information below and the booking form he completed and find **six** mistakes.

MODULE 15

Conditional sentences with *would*

would and *wouldn't*

1 Complete the sentences with *would* or *wouldn't*.

a I like working. If I didn't have a job, I ____would____ soon get bored.

b I'm very happy in the city: I _____ enjoy living in the country – it's too quiet!

c My sister is very honest. If she found some money in the street, I'm sure she _____ take it to the police.

d I _____ like to be famous: I'm quite happy as I am!

e Nobody has read the fire instructions: if there were a fire, they _____ know what to do.

f We can't go to Asia by bus because the journey _____ take much too long.

g If I could live my life again, I _____ change anything.

h It's a pity Mark isn't here. He _____ know what to do.

2 Put the verbs in brackets into the correct tense to make conditional sentences.

a I'm sorry, I don't know. If I _____knew_____ (know) the answer, I ___would tell___ (tell) you.

b If I _____ (not/work), we _____ (not/have) enough money to live.

c I'm sure you _____ (feel) better if you _____ (not/get up) so late.

d If you _____ (can) meet a famous person from history, who _____ (like) to talk to?

e I don't know what I _____ (do) if you _____ (be/not) here to help me.

f If I _____ (have) a lot of money, I _____ (take) you on an expensive holiday.

g If everyone _____ (speak) the same language, do you think life _____ (be) better?

h If you _____ (have) twenty brothers and sisters, think how many birthday presents you _____ (get)!

might or *would*

3 a Match the beginnings of the sentences in A with the endings in B.

A	B
1 He might help you	I'd go to Florida.
2 She wouldn't go out with him	if you were more polite to him.
3 If I could go on holiday anywhere in the world,	you might sleep better.
4 Robert might do better at school	if he didn't have so much money.
5 If you told her the truth,	if he did his homework regularly.
6 If you didn't drink so much coffee before going to bed,	she might get very angry.

b **T15.1** Listen and check. Practise saying the sentences.

4 Tick (✓) the correct sentence for each situation below.

1 Someone asks you to help them to translate a newspaper article into your language. Unfortunately, the newspaper article is in Chinese – a language you don't speak or understand. What do you say?
a *I'll help you if I can.*
b *I'd help if I could.* ✓

2 Someone asks about your plans for tomorrow. You're not sure yet – you're either going to the beach or to the cinema – it depends on the weather. What do you say?
a *If the weather's good, I'll go to the beach.*
b *If the weather was good, I'd go to the beach.*

3 You're on holiday at the seaside. The beach is very nice, but unfortunately the weather isn't very good – it's cloudy and the temperature is only 12°C. Someone asks if you're enjoying yourself. What do you say?
a *I'd be happier if the weather were better.*
b *I'll be happier if we have better weather.*

4 You invite a friend to go to a club with you, but she's got an exam tomorrow, so she can't come. What does she say to you?
a *I'll come if I don't have an exam.*
b *I'd come if I didn't have an exam.*

5 A taxi driver is driving you very slowly to the station. Your train leaves in five minutes. What do you say to him?
a *If we don't go faster, I'll miss the train.*
b *If we didn't go faster, I'd miss the train.*

6 A friend asks you to drive her home from a party, but your car is at home, so you can't help her. What do you say?
a *Sorry, if I have my car, I'll take you home.*
b *Sorry, if I had my car, I'd take you home.*

7 You see a child crossing the road reading a book. What do you say to the child?
a *If you're not careful, you'll have an accident.*
b *If you weren't careful, you'd have an accident.*

will and would

5 Circle the best form in each sentence, as in the example.

a I (wouldn't)/won't do that if I were you!
b Goodbye, everybody! *I'd/I'll* see you all next week.
c *I'd/I'll* help you if I had more time.
d What time *will/would* you be back from work this evening?
e I *won't/wouldn't* be surprised if they won the competition.
f Sorry, I can't speak now. *I'd/I'll* phone you back later.
g *I'll/I'd* be here until 6 o'clock if you need anything.
h Life *will/would* be so much easier if people worked together.
i If my mother were here, I'm sure *she'd/she'll* know what to do.

Short answers with *will* and *would*

> **Will** you / (s)he / it / we be at home?
> Yes, I / (s)he / it / we **will**.
> No, I / (s)he / it /we **won't**.
>
> **Would** you / (s)he / it / we work?
> Yes, I / (s)he / it / we **would**.
> No, I / (s)he / it / we **wouldn't**.

LOOK!

6 Write short answers to these questions.

a Would you travel to another planet if you had the opportunity? Yes, *I would.*
b Will your brother be at home if I phone this evening? No, _____ .
c Would you like to be Prime Minister of your country? No, _____ .
d Will we have time for lunch when we get there? Yes, _____ .
e If you won the lottery, would you give up work? Yes, _____ .
f Would you move to a bigger house if you had the money? No, _____ .
g If Kate and Roger get married, do you think they'll be happy? Yes, _____ .
h If a stranger offered you £1,000 to carry a bag onto an aeroplane, would you do it? No, _____ .

Vocabulary booster: people in politics, religion and public life

7 a Put the people in the box into the word map.

the Prime Minister   a communist   ~~a Catholic~~   a mayor   the President
a priest   the Vice President   a queen   a Buddhist   a social democrat
a king   a Muslim   a Member of Parliament   a judge   a Protestant
a government minister   a Christian   a Hindu   a green

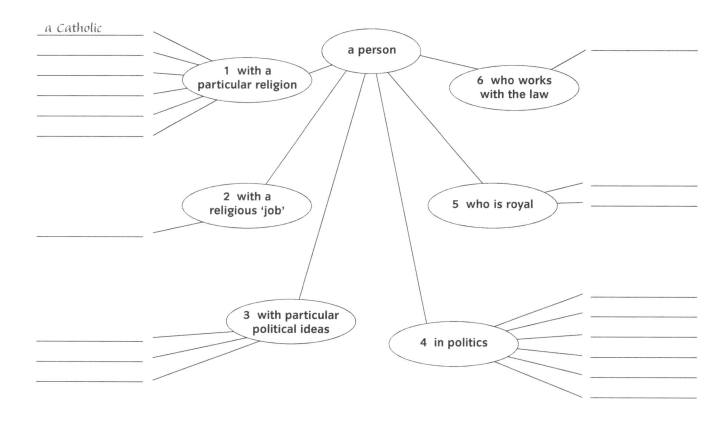

a Catholic

1 with a particular religion

a person

6 who works with the law

2 with a religious 'job'

5 who is royal

3 with particular political ideas

4 in politics

b **T15.2** Listen and practise the pronunciation of the words.

c **T15.3** Circle the correct answer in the general knowledge quiz below.
Listen and check your answers.

1 Mecca is a very important city for _Hindus / Muslims._

2 Lenin was a _communist / social democrat_ leader.

3 Rome is the centre of the _Protestant / Catholic_ church.

4 Margaret Thatcher was the first woman _Prime Minister / President_ of the United Kingdom.

5 The Netherlands has a _president / a queen._

6 The British Chancellor of the Exchequer is a _government minister / kind of priest._

7 Most people in India are _Hindus / Buddhists._

8 George Bush Senior was the _President / Prime Minister_ of the United States.

Listen and read

8 **T15.4** How many of the questions below can you answer?
Read and/or listen and check.

a Is a real Earth year longer or shorter than 365 days?
b Which is the lightest planet?
c Which planet was farthest from the Sun in 1995?
d What can be the size of a house?
e Which planet has the most moons?
f How long is a year on Mercury?
g What is twenty-seven kilometres high?
h Which planet is it possible to see without a telescope?
i What lasts for just under ten hours?
j Which planet has been mistaken for a UFO?
k How many Earths could the Sun hold?
l Which planet was discovered most recently?
m Which planet goes round the Sun 'lying down'?
n How many times has Neptune been round the Sun since it was discovered?

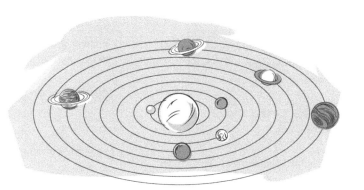

P **The Planets:** *did you know ...?*

The Sun is a star – it is not a planet. It is so big that you could fit more than one million Earths inside it. The Sun is the only star we see during the daytime.

Mercury is thirty-six million miles from the Sun and has no moons. It takes eighty-eight days to go round the Sun (at thirty miles per second), which means that there are fewer than two days in a year.

Venus is the closest planet to the Earth. It has a very hot surface and no moons. It is the brightest planet and can sometimes be seen with the naked eye if you know where to look. It is sometimes the cause of UFO reports.

The Earth is orbited by one moon and is ninety-three million miles away from the Sun. The average year is actually 365 days, five hours, forty-eight minutes and 45.51 seconds. Three quarters of the Earth is covered by water.

Mars is a cold, red, rocky planet with two very small moons which orbit close to the surface. It is the home of the 'Olympus Mons', the largest volcano found in the solar system. It is twenty-seven kilometres high and its crater is eight-one kilometres wide.

Jupiter is the largest planet in the solar system, with sixteen moons. It spins very quickly on its axis, and one day lasts nine hours and fifty-five minutes.

Saturn has eighteen moons and is over 800 million miles from the Earth. It is the second biggest planet but also the lightest. If there was a bath big enough to hold Saturn, it would float in the water. It has rings round it made of ice: the particles of ice vary in size from a grain of sugar to a house.

Uranus is a giant gas planet which is over one billion miles away and has fifteen moons. Its axis is at a ninety-seven degree angle, which means it orbits lying on its side – talk about a lazy planet!

Neptune is a giant gas planet and has eight moons. It was discovered in 1846, but has still not made a complete orbit of the Sun. One Neptune year lasts 165 Earth years.

Pluto is over three billion miles from the Sun and has one moon. It is the farthest planet from the Sun, but sometimes its orbit brings it closer to the Sun than Neptune: from 1989 to 1999 it jumped ahead of Neptune, then went back to being the farthest. Pluto is the only planet that has not been visited by a spacecraft. Because it is so small, it was not discovered until 1930.

Glossary
UFO = an unidentified flying object

Spelling
Silent 'w'

9 a Sometimes the letter 'w' is silent. Which of the 'w's below are silent?

would	wrong	whole
weight	when	walk	answer
why	songwriter	whose
worried	wrote	

b **T15.5** Listen and cross out the silent 'w's.

c Complete the rules below with examples from part a.

1 If a word begins with **wr**, 'w' is always silent, for example _____ .

2 If a word begins with **wh**, 'w' is usually silent, for example _____ .

3 A few other words have a silent 'w', for example _____ .

Pronunciation
The sound /w/

10 **T15.6** Listen and practise the /w/ pronunciation in these words and phrases from module 15.

will	won't
words	wouldn't
world	war
whites	wife
woman	weekend
to wonder	working

Improve your writing
Error correction (2)

11 Here is a student's letter for the Optional writing activity on page 137 of the Students' book. The teacher has marked 22 mistakes, using the following code:

Sp for a spelling mistake
P for a punctuation mistake
WW for a wrong word.

Write the corrections below.

Planet Hero

Hello everybody!

Here we are! We've finally arrived and I'm ¹writeing [Sp] to you from the Planet Hero!

There's enough oxygen and lots of plants, but ²fortunately [WW] the weather isn't very good and ³its [Sp] rained every day so far – as you can see it isn't all that ⁴diferent [Sp] from life in ⁵england [P]!

The journey was very, very long – ten weeks on a spaceship – ⁶then [WW] it was quite ⁷boreing [Sp] at times. I read all the books ⁸what [WW] you gave me during the first week, ⁹but [WW] I had to watch Space TV instead.

The other six people here are all very nice: one of them is a ¹⁰docter [Sp] from ¹¹france [P] – his ¹²names [P] ¹³rené [P].

Today we met our first Herovian (¹⁴thats [P] the name for the people ¹⁵which [WW] live here) and guess what? He speaks ¹⁶english [P]!

This morning I saw a small green person ¹⁷siting [Sp] on a wall, looking at me.

'Hello,' I ¹⁸sayed [Sp], 'what's your name ¹⁹; [P]'

²⁰Fine, thanks, [P] he answered, and ran away.

Anyway, it's ²¹geting [Sp] late, so I'd better go to bed. Give my love to all my ²²frends [Sp] and family.

Simona

1 _____	9 _____	17 _____
2 _____	10 _____	18 _____
3 _____	11 _____	19 _____
4 _____	12 _____	20 _____
5 _____	13 _____	21 _____
6 _____	14 _____	22 _____
7 _____	15 _____	
8 _____	16 _____	

Pronunciation table

Consonants		Vowels	
Symbol	Key Word	Symbol	Key Word
p	**p**an	iː	b**ea**t
b	**b**an	ɪ	b**i**t
t	**t**ip	e	b**e**t
d	**d**ip	æ	b**a**t
k	**c**ap	ɑː	b**ar**
g	**g**ap	ɒ	bl**o**ck
tʃ	**church**	ɔː	b**ough**t
dʒ	**judge**	ʊ	b**oo**k
f	**f**ew	uː	b**oo**t
v	**v**iew	ʌ	b**u**t
θ	**th**row	ɜː	b**ur**n
ð	**th**ough	ə	broth**er**
s	**s**ip	eɪ	b**ay**
z	**z**ero	əʊ	b**o**ne
ʃ	fre**sh**	aɪ	b**y**
ʒ	mea**s**ure	aʊ	b**ou**nd
h	**h**ot	ɔɪ	b**oy**
m	su**m**	ɪə	b**eer**
n	su**n**	eə	b**are**
ŋ	su**ng**	ʊə	p**oor**
l	**l**ot	eɪə	pl**ay**er
r	**r**ot	əʊə	l**ow**er
j	**y**et	aɪə	t**ire**
w	**w**et	aʊə	fl**ow**er
		ɔɪə	empl**oy**er
		i	happ**y**
		u	ann**u**al

Special signs

/ˈ/ shows main stress

/ˌ/ shows secondary stress

/ə/ means that /ə/ may or may not be used

Pearson Education Limited

Edinburgh Gate

Harlow

Essex CM20 2JE

England

and Associated Companies throughout the world.

www.longman.com/cuttingedge

First published 2005

Fifteenth impression 2023

ISBN-13: 978-0-582-82512-3

ISBN-10: 0-582-82512-1

Set in 9pt Stone Informal

Printed in Great Britain by Ashford Colour Press Ltd.

Acknowledgements

The author would like to thank Jonathan Tennant and everyone at International House Sydney for their support and advice.

Photo Acknowledgements

We are grateful to the following for permission to reproduce photographs:

BBC: page 16 (bottom right); Camera Press: page 47 (Patrick Baldwin), page 74 (Yannis Vlamos); Corbis: page 44 (top right) (Yoram Kahanal), page 54 (Mel Yates), page 64 (Horace Bristol 1946); Eye Ubiquitous/Hutchinson: page 6, page 28 (top right) (bottom right) (Lib Taylor) Freemantle Media Ltd: page 16 (top right); Getty Images: page 12, page 44 (top left), page 52 (Stone); Robert Harding: page 37; Kobal Collection: page 16 (left); PowerStock/SuperStock Ltd: page 31; D C Williamson London: page 28 (bottom left).

The cover photograph has been kindly supplied by Getty Images/Image Bank.

Every effort has been made to trace the copyright holders and we apologise in advance for any unintentional omissions. We would be pleased to insert the appropriate acknowledgement in any subsequent edition of this publication.

Picture research by Andrea Sadler/Sandra Hilsdon

Illustrated by Colin Brown, Kes Hankin (Gemini Design), Andy Hammond, Connie Jude, Tim Kahane, Chris Pavely, Theresa Tibberts, Mark Vallance (Gemini Design)

Designed by Jennifer Coles

Project Managed by Lindsay White